The Master's Degree:
Tradition, Diversity, Innovation

by Judith S. Glazer

ASHE-ERIC Higher Education Report No. 6, 1986

Prepared by

 ® *Clearinghouse on Higher Education*
The George Washington University

Published by

Association for the Study of Higher Education

Jonathan D. Fife,
Series Editor

Cite as
Glazer, Judith S. *The Master's Degree: Tradition, Diversity, Innovation.* ASHE-ERIC Higher Education Report No. 6. Washington, D.C.: Association for the Study of Higher Education, 1986.

Cover design by Michael David Brown, Inc., Rockville, MD.

The ERIC Clearinghouse on Higher Education invites individuals to submit proposals for writing monographs for the Higher Education Report series. Proposals must include:
1. A detailed manuscript proposal of not more than five pages.
2. A 75-word summary to be used by several review committees for the initial screening and rating of each proposal.
3. A vita.
4. A writing sample.

Library of Congress Catalog Card Number 86-72855
ISSN 0884-0040
ISBN 0-913317-33-0

ERIC® **Clearinghouse on Higher Education**
The George Washington University
One Dupont Circle, Suite 630
Washington, D.C. 20036

ASHE **Association for the Study of Higher Education**
One Dupont Circle, Suite 630
Washington, D.C. 20036

Office of Educational
Research and Improvement
U.S. Department of Education

This publication was partially prepared with funding from the Office of Educational Research and Improvement, U.S. Department of Education, under contract no. 400-86-0017. The opinions expressed in this report do not necessarily reflect the positions or policies of OERI or the Department.

EXECUTIVE SUMMARY

The master's degree has been shaped by the traditional arts and science model as the first postbaccalaureate degree conferred upon candidates following one year of graduate study. It is the mid-point to the doctorate, the terminal degree for most professions, and a source of enrichment in the chosen field of study. It exceeds other graduate degrees in its diversity, validating successful completion of a program in numerous disciplines and subfields of study. This report reviews the research on the development of the master's degree in the United States and its growth in the postwar technological era within the context of tradition, diversity, and change. It synthesizes research on structure and organization, curricular reform, quality control, and innovation, concluding with recommendations for future research.

What Is the Current Status of the Master's Degree?

In 1982–83, 289,921 master's degrees in 30 disciplines and 633 specialties were conferred, an increase of 75 percent in the past two decades (OERI 1985). Professional master's degrees accounted for 84.2 percent of the total, liberal arts master's degrees for 15.8 percent. Nearly three times as many master's degrees were conferred in 1982–83 as the aggregate of first professional and doctoral degrees, and more than half of them were awarded in education and business. Teacher education, once the major field partly because of its certifying role, has declined as a percentage of total degrees awarded. Business, health sciences, computer science, psychology, and public affairs are now the fastest-growing fields of study (OERI 1985). No longer can the graduate school, confronted by new professional programs seeking autonomy from the research model, function effectively as an academic "Bureau of Standards" (Pelikan 1983). It is increasingly difficult to define universities in terms of scholarly research, because a myriad of professional degrees now overshadow the arts and sciences as terminal credentials facilitating access and advancement in the marketplace. Demands for quality control, accountability, and standards are countered by proposals for innovation, change, and the implementation of new graduate programs (Pelczar and Solmon 1984). State education boards, accrediting agencies, and professional associations comment with increasing frequency on the problems of the proliferation of degrees, while institutions mount efforts to attract nontraditional clienteles to existing and new degree programs. The result is uncertainty about the role of the university and the functions and purposes of graduate and professional education and about the meaning of a generic degree of such diversity that no single definition adequately describes its structure, content, and goals.

How Diversified Is the Master's Degree?

No single master's degree exists, and its diversity has been a source of concern throughout this century (Spurr 1970). The multiplicity and variety of professional programs, combined with persistent efforts to differentiate these degrees from the dominant arts and science model, have resulted in an avalanche of new titles (OERI 1985). Curricular models reflect this diversity; they vary widely in emphasis but generally include five major components—introductory core courses, a major concentration in a subfield or specialty, cognate or elective courses to expand and strengthen the program, an integrative experience, and a summative experience. Master's degrees are classified as academic, professional, or experiential, making comparisons difficult. Each discipline may have more than one designation or title, numerous fields, subfields, or concentrations, variable requirements for credit, different levels of degrees, and different integrative and summative experiences. Efforts to conceptualize the master's degree falter amid the continued proliferation of this level of program development by professional groups and within institutions themselves. It is only in the past decade that attention has been given to the important role of professional schools, the nature of graduate education in the professions, and the extraordinary diversification of the master's degree in certifying professional achievement in a variety of areas (CGS 1979; Spurr 1970). In an effort to bridge the gap between professional and nonprofessional disciplines, it may be that the new paradigm of graduate education is the first professional degree—a highly differentiated degree whose content and structure are based on more utilitarian and measurable objectives and directed toward more immediate outcomes that reflect contemporary societal values. The issue is not the devaluation of the baccalaureate or the master of arts, but the new dominance of professionalism at all levels, associate through doctoral degree.

How Are Standards Maintained?
The past two decades have witnessed an ongoing dialogue over how quality should be assessed. In graduate and professional education, the master's degree has received little attention, but recent research indicates that neither reputational rankings nor quantitative assessments are adequate and that multidimensional indicators are needed to assess this level of degree. The accrediting process has focused on two concerns—educational quality and institutional integrity, attempting to discourage proliferation and specialization, to define and monitor quality within specific disciplines, and to measure educational outcomes. States have reviewed academic programs as a means of coordinating, assessing, and consolidating graduate programs. State oversight is more prevalent in public than in private universities, and it is characterized by two kinds of problems: the diversity of programs, which makes generic criteria difficult to sustain, and the perceived need for public institutions in particular to respond to the needs of non-traditional clienteles (Pelczar and Solmon 1984). In an effort to systematize the review of master's level programs, the Council of Graduate Schools and the Graduate Record Examination Board have devised the Graduate Program Self-Assessment Service for institutional self-study of programs or departments.

What Are the Dominant Models?
The major professional degrees range from business, engineering, and public affairs to teacher education, nursing, and library science, and they include many specialties within each degree designation. The overriding issue in the literature on these degrees is the dilemma between theory and practice—how to balance the need for practical knowledge and training in a skill with the theoretical framework of the field of study. The major issues are specialization or multidisciplinary education, requirements for admission and for the degree, access and standards, and modes of instruction and delivery. The inroads being made by corporate colleges and other noncollegiate alternatives are a source of concern within the academic community (Hug-

stad 1983). Business alone spends an estimated $40 to 60 billion a year on management training, much of it comparable to advanced degree programs.

Is There Room for Innovation?
In the 1960s and early 1970s, change was a function of the rapid expansion of graduate education, the vocationalism of graduate students, and the introduction of public policies to strengthen access and opportunity at all levels. Today, in a climate of retrenchment, change is linked to the management of enrollments, to the market for jobs, and to adherence to external and institutional standards. Graduate and professional schools are seeking to respond to society's and individuals' perceived needs and are encountering limited incentives with which to implement new programs and demands from state and accreditation agencies for higher standards, greater productivity, and more measurable outcomes (Folger 1984). Disincentives to change go beyond the costs and benefits of implementing new programs—to continuing preference for theoretical over applied programs, vertical specialization over breadth, and established over emergent programs in the status hierarchy (Pelczar and Solmon 1984). External degrees, experiential learning, cooperative education, interinstitutional consortia, combined degrees, interdisciplinary programs, and distance learning are some of the mechanisms and strategies being implemented in graduate and professional programs with mixed results. It is evident that innovation and change will require both leadership from administrators and support from faculty and that graduate and professional education must respond to the needs of nontraditional postbaccalaureate students seeking professional advancement as well as personal enrichment.

A concerted effort is needed to focus on the master's degree—its academic strengths and weaknesses, its diffuse character, and its importance in the hierarchy of degrees. The master's degree is distinct from other graduate degrees and needs to be analyzed as a class of degrees rather than as one generic model. While its relationship to the baccalaureate and doctorate is important, it is increasingly sought as a credential on its own merits. By addressing the issues pervading this degree, we can modify and adapt various models that strengthen postbaccalaureate education and suggest future parameters for the master's degree.

ADVISORY BOARD

Roger G. Baldwin
Assistant Professor of Education
College of William and Mary

Susan W. Cameron
Assistant Professor and Chair
Higher/Postsecondary Education Program
Syracuse University

Clifton F. Conrad
Professor of Higher Education
University of Arizona

Elaine H. El-Khawas
Vice President
Policy Analysis and Research
American Council on Education

George D. Kuh
Associate Dean for Academic Affairs
School of Education
Indiana University

David W. Leslie
Professor and Chair
Department of Educational Leadership
Florida State University

Yvonna S. Lincoln
Associate Professor of Higher Education
University of Kansas

CONSULTING EDITORS

Paul A. Albrecht
Executive Vice President and Dean
Claremont Graduate School

G. Lester Anderson
Professor Emeritus
Pennsylvania State University

Robert C. Andringa
President
Creative Solutions

John B. Bennett
Director
Office on Self-Regulation
American Council on Education

Carole J. Bland
Associate Professor
Department of Family Practice and Community Health
University of Minnesota

Judith A. Clementson-Mohr
Director of Psychological Services
Purdue University

Mark H. Curtis
President Emeritus
Association of American Colleges

Martin Finkelstein
Associate Professor of Higher Education Administration
Seton Hall University

Andrew T. Ford
Provost and Dean of College
Allegheny College

Roderick S. French
Vice President for Academic Affairs
George Washington University

Timothy Gallineau
Vice President for Student Development
Saint Bonaventure University

G. Manuel Gunne
Adjunct Associate Professor
College of Nursing
University of Utah

James C. Hearn
Associate Professor
Department of Educational Policy and Administration
University of Minnesota

Dennis H. Holmes
Associate Professor
Department of Education
George Washington University

Jules B. LaPidus
President
Council of Graduate Schools in the United States

Arthur S. Marmaduke
Director
Eureka Project

Richard M. Millard
President
Council on Postsecondary Accreditation

L. Jackson Newell
Professor and Dean
University of Utah

Steven G. Olswang
Assistant Provost for Academic Affairs
University of Washington

Patricia Rueckel
Executive Director
National Association for Women Deans,
    Administrators, and Counselors

John P. Sciacca
Assistant Professor
Department of Health, Physical Education, and Recreation
Northern Arizona University

Richard F. Stevens
Executive Director
National Association of Student Personnel Administrators

Thomas R. Wolanin
Staff Director
Subcommittee on Postsecondary Education
United States House of Representatives

FOREWORD

The master's degree is going through an identity crisis. In an era of increased specialization, employer demands, student expectations for practicality, and external calls for accountability, academe cannot afford to let this state of affairs continue. Some hard questions must be asked. What is the primary function of a master's degree? How can it best serve the demands of students, employers, and governing bodies?

This report examines the educational mission or function of a master's degree. Today's master's serves one of three objectives: (1) as a stepping stone to a doctorate; (2) as a consolation prize for those who are unwilling or unable to continue; or (3) as a terminal degree for many professions. The degree certifies a certain level of proficiency. It can embody theoretical understanding as well as technical expertise. It is important to keep the differences in mind when evaluating the curricula of master's programs.

Curriculum content and design must be addressed carefully. Is a master's degree merely a collection of courses approximate to one year beyond the baccalaureate? Or is there an attempt to carefully weigh or give balance to theory and skill courses? To what degree have master's programs been evaluated in a way that measures the success of stated objectives?

Any evaluation should imply a concern for quality. Of any degree, the master's should probably be given the closest scrutiny since it is the one most often attained by part-time students in off-campus programs, which are harder to regulate. As adults continue to go back periodically for more education, there will be greater emphasis on and expectations for the master's, and greater demand for accountability. College and university reputations, if not survival, will be influenced by their master's programs.

Judith Glazer, associate dean of the School of Education and Human Services at St. John's University in New York, establishes the importance of examining master's programs by noting that "in 1982–83, 289,921 master's degrees in 30 disciplines and 633 specialties were conferred, an increase of 75 percent in the past two decades." She presents a fine assessment of quality measurement and control, as well as a useful overview of different professional degrees. Perhaps her greatest contribution is the compilation and differentiation of the various degrees offered under the guise of master's programs.

Administrators and faculty will do well to examine the range and diversity of master's degrees offered, keeping in mind that adult learners will continue to be mainstays of colleges and universities well into the next century. Serving these "new" students well will be vital to higher education institutions. The master's degree has traditionally been the closest link between academe and business, and the skills demanded by a changing workforce will reinforce this traditional arrangement. This report can help some institutions better serve the next generations of graduate students.

Jonathan D. Fife
Series Editor
Director and Professor
ERIC Clearinghouse on Higher Education
The George Washington University

ACKNOWLEDGMENTS

I wish to thank Robert Raymo for his support throughout
the preparation of this manuscript. His knowledge and
judgment have been invaluable. Many individuals
responded to my requests for data, and I want to acknowledge their assistance and cooperation, particularly the
directors and staffs of state higher education boards and
national accreditation agencies and the reference librarians
of New York University and St. John's University who
conducted valuable searches of scholarly material on my
behalf. I also thank Vance Grant, Jules LaPidus, David
Webster, and my editor, Jonathan Fife, for their generous
assistance.

INTRODUCTION

The master's degree is the mainspring of graduate education, the first postbaccalaureate degree, the midpoint to the doctorate—and the terminal degree for most professions. Beyond this generalization, little agreement exists about its goals and objectives, functions and purposes, curricula, and criteria for evaluation. It exceeds other graduate degrees in number and diversity, ranging from the traditional Master of Arts and the first professional Master of Business Administration to experiential and combined degrees. It is at once a mechanism for awarding credentials, a stimulus to research and scholarship, and a generator of enrollments and tuition income. In the past quarter century, it has altered greatly, expanding in response to societal needs, public policy initiatives, interests of administrators and faculty, and demands from various constituencies. In a highly technological environment, the master's degree has become a means of certifying successful completion of professional programs that prepare students for careers in the public and private sectors. At the same time, it maintains its traditional function of initiating graduate students into the academic milieu of research and scholarship.

The conferral of master's degrees has risen by 75 percent in the past 20 years, reaching a high of 317,164 in 1976–77.

Of the 3,253 colleges and universities in the United States, 1,207 offer graduate programs (Grant and Snyder 1983, p. 105). Most master's degrees continue to be offered by the institutions that grant doctoral degrees (452 institutions offer both degrees); 523 offer the master's and 93 the first professional as the highest degrees, and 139 offer degrees beyond the master's but below the doctorate. Of the 523 master's degree institutions, 157 are public and 366 are private.

The conferral of master's degrees has risen by 75 percent in the past 20 years, reaching a high of 317,164 in 1976–77. In 1982–83, 289,921 master's degrees were conferred in 30 disciplines, subdivided into 633 specialties (see table 1). Professional master's degrees accounted for 84.2 percent of the total, liberal arts master's degrees for 15.8 percent.

Nearly three times as many master's degrees were conferred in 1982–83 as the aggregate of first professional (law, medicine, theology) and doctoral degrees. More than half of all master's degrees were awarded in education and business, which have grown much faster than the number of science and engineering degrees (NSF 1982, p. 13). Sci-

TABLE 1
MASTER'S DEGREES CONFERRED: 1982–83

	Number of Degrees	Number of Subfields	Percent of Total Degrees
Professional			
Agriculture/Natural Resources	4,254	67	1.5
Architecture/Environmental Design	3,357	8	1.2
Area/Ethnic Studies	826	20	.3
Business/Management	65,319	45	22.5
Communications and Communications Technologies	3,602	12	1.2
Computer/Information Science	5,321	6	1.8
Education	84,853	63	29.3
Engineering and Engineering Technologies	19,350	45	6.7
Health Sciences	17,068	104	5.9
Home Economics	2,406	33	.8
Law	2,091	4	.7
Library/Archival Sciences	3,979	5	1.4
Military Sciences	110	4	.0
Parks/Recreation	565	5	.2
Protective Services	1,300	11	.5
Public Affairs	16,245	10	5.6
Theology	4,782	2	1.6
Visual/Performing Arts	8,742	38	3.0
Total	244,170	482	84.2
Academic			
Foreign Languages	1,759	25	.6
Letters	5,767	12	2.0
Liberal/General Studies	889	2	.3
Life Sciences	5,696	30	2.0
Mathematics	2,837	6	1.0
Multi/Interdisciplinary Studies	2,930	8	1.0
Philosophy/Religion	1,091	11	.4
Physical Sciences	5,290	31	1.8
Psychology	8,378	13	2.9
Social Sciences	11,114	13	3.8
Total	45,751	151	15.8
Grand Total	289,921	633	100.0

Sources: NCES 1985; OERI 1985.

ence and engineering degrees reached a high of 30 percent of all master's degrees in 1965 but have declined to about 18 percent in the past decade. Nationally, an average of 300 master's degrees are awarded per institution, although this figure is much higher at major universities.

Teacher education, once the dominant field (partly because of its role in certification and licensing), has declined as a percentage of total degrees awarded. In 1962, 45 percent of all master's degrees were in education, compared to 6.5 percent in business. Twenty years later, 29.3 percent were awarded in education and 22.5 percent in business (OERI 1985). Engineering, which was second with 11 percent in 1962, dropped to third with 6.7 percent in 1982–83. While enrollments have fallen, types of education degrees have risen in recent years. Sixty-three specializations in education are included in the new taxonomy on earned degrees (OERI 1985).[1] Characteristics of students have also changed. In 1982–83, women received 50.2 percent and minorities 10.5 percent of all master's degrees. Although historically women have been the major recipients of degrees in education and the health sciences, they are opting in greater numbers for such traditionally male-dominated fields as business and management.

The distribution of degrees by level has remained fairly constant since 1930 (Adkins 1971; Plisko and Stern 1985). The proportion of bachelor's and second-level degrees over the 40 years of Adkins's study of academic degree production from 1930 to 1970 was approximately three to one—73 percent bachelor's to 25 percent master's and first professional. In 1981, 70 percent of all degrees were bachelor's, 27.5 percent master's and first professional (Grant and Snyder 1983, p. 132). Between 1972–73 and 1982–83, the number of master's degrees conferred increased 9 percent (OERI 1985); compared to a 44 percent increase in first professional degrees, a 5 percent increase in bachelor's degrees, and a 6 percent decline in doctoral degrees. The conferral of degrees has moved gradually toward business, education, psychology, engineering, and computer

1. Beginning in 1982–83, the taxonomy used by the Office of Educational Research and Improvement (formerly NCES) to collect data on earned degrees was revised, and the number of reportable subfields more than doubled, from 308 to 633 (OERI 1985).

science, with the rapidly growing fields increasing from 15 to 41 percent of degree holders from 1930 to 1970. The most rapidly growing fields at the master's level are now business, health sciences, computer science, psychology, and public affairs (OERI 1985). Foreign languages, letters, library science, mathematics, and social sciences have seen major declines.

Several issues arise in reviewing research on this vital aspect of higher education. The ebb and flow of institutional and governmental subsidies have left graduate and professional education generally without a stable base on which to articulate the master's degree (Brademas 1983, p. 39; NBGE 1975). This situation is exacerbated by the changing patterns in undergraduates' majors and the trend toward early specialization (Grant and Snyder 1983, p. 118). In consequence, the Master of Arts and Master of Science degrees occupy a position between the baccalaureate and the doctorate that is often tenuous and ill defined.

No longer can the graduate school, confronted by new professional programs seeking autonomy from the research model of graduate schools, function effectively as an academic "Bureau of Standards" (Pelikan 1983, p. 13). It becomes increasingly inappropriate and misleading to define universities in terms of their scholarly and academic research when myriads of professional degrees now overshadow the arts and sciences as terminal credentials facilitating access to and advancement in the marketplace. Demands for quality control, accountability, and standards are countered by proposals for innovation, change, and the introduction of new graduate programs (Albrecht 1984; Pelikan 1983). State coordinating boards, national accreditation agencies, and regional associations monitor with ever greater vigilance the proliferation of programs. Institutions, in their efforts to attract students, compete with corporations, school systems, and proprietary schools in degree and nondegree programs. The result is confusion and uncertainty about the role of the university, the purpose of graduate and professional education, and the function of a generic degree of such diversity that no single definition adequately describes its structure, content, and goals. A crisis of confidence exists: Are graduate and professional schools capable of monitoring the quality of master's degrees or attuned to their multiple purposes? (Giamatti 1981, p. 141).

This report reviews the research on the development of the master's degree in the United States and its growth in the postwar technological era within the context of tradition, diversity, and change. It synthesizes research on structure and organization, the reform of curricula, quality control, and innovation, concluding with recommendations for future research.

HISTORICAL DEVELOPMENTS

The degree is entrenched in the culture of American post-secondary education, part of the dogma through which the academic system legitimizes its missions and purposes and perpetuates itself. It is linked inextricably to the ritual of graduation, conferred in a ceremony marking the recipient's rite of passage into the world of work. It is what the degree symbolizes that gives it its intrinsic merit (Eels 1963). Where it is obtained provides tangible proof of the value and benefits of the academic experience. While the degree that originated in the thirteenth century was originally a license to teach and afterward became an obligation to teach, its implications are now more important than the title it carries (Eels 1963; Spurr 1970). The title has become a generic label that describes in the broadest terms the level at which it was granted and in specific terms the functions that the recipient is eligible to perform.

In America, the practice of conferring degrees was introduced at Harvard University in 1642 for young men seeking teaching careers, generally in divinity (Eels 1963, p. 73). [The English medieval university had granted this second degree following professional study in theology, law, and medicine since the thirteenth century (Storr 1953, p. 1).] The following year it instituted the first scholarship for a student seeking the Master of Arts degree. Although it conferred the master's on five of the nine members of its first graduating class in 1649, there was little incentive to pursue it, as it did not qualify the recipient for a profession or enhance his education beyond the baccalaureate (Storr 1953, p. 2). It was granted "as a matter of course" (in cursu) rather than as an earned degree to candidates of good moral character who had taken the bachelor's degree at the college, paid fees for three years, and spent a year of additional study in residence under the guidance of a "master teacher" (Spurr 1970, p. 12). In 1734, these requirements were expanded to include a thesis and its defense and demonstrated fluency in Latin and Greek (Eels 1963, p. 74).

With the foundation of schools and colleges throughout the South and Midwest following passage of the Morrill Act in 1862, the demand for public school and college teachers grew (Berelson 1960). Interest in scientific research spurred the establishment of new universities based on continental models where higher education culminated in the doctorate (Berelson 1960; Giamatti 1981; Veysey 1965). It was in this context that in 1851 Henry Tappan, president of the University of Michigan, conceptualized a new model for the American university based on a combined English-German model (Spurr 1970, p. 12), instituting the Master of Arts and Master of Science as earned degrees (pro meritis) in a symbiotic relationship with the baccalaureate and the doctorate. Michigan conferred the first earned M.A. in 1859 (Spurr 1970, p. 13).

The earned master's degree flourished in the last 30 years of the nineteenth century and beyond. Its growth as an earned degree can be attributed to several factors, among them the expansion of doctoral education, philanthropic support of basic research, the demand for teachers, the advent of coeducation, and the emergence of undergraduate general education (at Harvard and elsewhere), which required the introduction of a second course of study beyond the bachelor's for the higher degree of Master of Arts or Science (Snell 1965, p. 75; Storr 1953, p. 125). It was usually granted following one year of full-time study and completion of an examination and a thesis, but certain professional degrees in applied fields demanded two years of graduate study. The requirement for an examination, which appears to have been universal in the nineteenth century, fell into disuse in the early twentieth (AAU 1910).

The establishment of the Association of American Universities (AAU) in 1900 marked the beginning of a national movement to consolidate and standardize developments in higher education (Berelson 1960; Spurr 1970). Presidents of prestigious universities and graduate deans deplored the lack of quality of the master's degree. With each decade, they found it to need more radical rehabilitation and regularly took the occasion of the association's annual meetings to observe how little the degree meant to students embarked on the path toward the doctorate. Recommendations were made to improve its quality, always, however, from the perspective of arts and science, rarely from that of the professions, which even then accounted for the majority of master's degrees.

The AAU commissioned the first major study of the master's degree in 1909 to determine whether the master's should be structured as a research degree, emphasizing scholarly investigation, as a prerequisite for certification of secondary school teachers, or as a cultural degree for enrichment. Dean Calvin Thomas of Columbia University presented its results at the 1910 annual meeting; he found little standardization of requirements for either admission or the degree. The degree titles, M.A., M.S., and M.Phil., were used interchangeably, depending on the antecedent degree. The disparity between requirements for residence, the conflicting policies on specialization, the absence of articulation between undergraduate and graduate programs, the dubious practice of correspondence and extension credits—all were severely criticized. Thomas concluded caustically, "If we could get rid of that feeling which a pathologist might call the pergamental psychosis, if there were no such thing as graduation, if the young person left college at his convenience, carrying no visible trophy save a plain unvarnished record of his performance in the several studies pursued, many of our present difficulties would melt away as if by magic" (AAU 1910, p. 34).

In 1909, the AAU began to define what constituted a proper department, course, college, school, division, and curriculum, and for the next 40 years, it served as the arbiter of academic standards for graduate education. It was not until 1935, however, that its Committee on Problems Relating to the Master's Degree issued a comprehensive report on the degree's purposes, nomenclature, and standards (AAU 1935, p. 32). It described the master's as a "research degree, a professional degree, a teacher's degree, and a culture degree," and it recommended one year of graduate study in a unified program of graduate courses, culminating in a final examination and original thesis. (At the time, only one-half of AAU members required either an examination or a thesis, the prevailing requirement being one year of course work based on state regulations for secondary school teachers.) The committee also sought to stem the tide of new degree titles, affirming that the M.A. and M.S. were the appropriate designations, with qualifying phrase if needed, and to check the growth of professional degrees. By then, the master's degree carried financial rewards; many universities introduced shortcuts to its completion, including correspondence courses, extension work, and summer programs for teachers and school administrators, practices the AAU deplored (AAU 1927, p. 108).

As World War II ended, the number of master's degrees increased eighteenfold. The AAU Committee on Graduate Work issued a strong report on standards for the degree, including a recommendation to identify different types of master's degrees by separate designations—the M.A. and M.S. as research degrees, the M.A.T. and M.Ed. as teaching degrees, and technical degrees with a qualifying phrase (AAU 1945, p. 124). Professional meetings and commission reports in the fifties continually complained of the

> *deplorable state of the M.A., the failure of recruiting programs, the inordinate lag between the B.A. and Ph.D., the lack of articulation between undergraduate and graduate work, the controversy over the language requirement, the unsatisfactory situation with respect to qualifying and final examinations, the nature and length of the dissertation, the structure and organization of graduate schools, and so on ad infinitum* (Carmichael 1961, p. 3).

As a former university and foundation president, Carmichael devised a plan for a three-year master's degree to prepare teachers for community colleges and the lower division of four-year colleges. About 75,000 master's degrees were conferred in 1959–60, and only 40 percent of college faculty had Ph.D.s. At that time, 150 master's degree designations were available, mostly technical and vocational, and both the master's and the doctorate were becoming more professionalized, less scholarly, and available in fields other than liberal arts (p. 8). The proposal was made in response to the Association of Graduate Schools's (AGS) admonition in 1959 for a "master's degree, rehabilitated, revitalized, resuscitated, redefined, and readjusted." The Fund for the Advancement of Education, a division of the Ford Foundation, supported pilot programs. Undergraduates in the highest 15 to 20 percent of their class combined the two upper division years with one year of graduate study, receiving an M.Phil. The program attracted able students, but they tended to continue to pursue the Ph.D. rather than to stop with the master's. The M.Phil. was perceived as a pallid substitute for someone who had completed all requirements for a Ph.D. but the dissertation, and failed. In the final analysis, the academic establishment preferred faculty with doctorates to M.Phil.s (Spurr 1970, p. 72).

A later attempt by Yale University to replace the M.A. and M.S. with the M.Phil. met with little success, and by 1972, its faculty voted for reinstatement of the traditional master's degrees (CGS 1977, p. 147; Miller 1966). Today, many graduate schools routinely award the M.Phil. to doctoral candidates upon completion of all requirements for candidacy except the dissertation.

In a special issue of the *Journal of Higher Education* on problems and policies in graduate education, Elder (1959, p. 135) proposed that master's programs be devised de novo rather than appended to doctorates like poor cousins or offered "consolationis causa." He suggested an 18-month program, to include research, an integrative seminar, supervised college teaching, a scholarly essay, and proficiency in a foreign language. Blegen (1959, p. 131) took an opposite view, arguing that it was "absurd to suppose that the multiform and multipurpose master's degree can or should be replaced by some new and rehabilitated master's degree." In a similar vein, it was observed later that the master's did not need rehabilitation so much as rigor (Snell 1965, p. 101).

In 1960, the master's degree suffered from two major problems—diversity and decline in prestige (Berelson 1960). The dilemma was its relative strength in liberal arts colleges and universities, where it was the highest degree, compared to its conspicuous weakness in research universities dominated by doctoral faculty and learned societies. Berelson was pessimistic about its elevation into a respected, research-oriented, two-year degree for college teachers. "There is too much going against it: its historical decline, the lower prestige, the diversity of meaning, the competitive disadvantage relative to the doctorate, the coolness of better colleges, the reluctance of the better students, the poorer career prospects, the low return on investment" (p. 189). Although the degree was essential for "certifying, testing, and consoling" and while it carried its weight in "the academic procession," no amount of reform would make it into a prestigious degree then or ever.

As World War II ended, the number of master's degrees increased eighteenfold.

Nevertheless, the professional master's degree continued to flourish in the 1960s and 1970s. Professional schools enjoyed a rapid turnover, large enrollments, income from tuition, and external support from various constituencies; federal and state grants provided fellowships and facilities for doctoral study and research. As doctoral programs expanded, however, the liberal arts master's degree was further devalued and became for all intents and purposes a credential offered at the conclusion of first-year graduate work, not a research degree but an introduction to a field of study. Other trends contributed to its declining status: increased emphasis on advanced study for teachers, calling into question its use to certify college faculty, the impact of federal policies on service professions that now required advanced degrees, the growth of graduate programs in business and engineering, and the second-class status of master's degree recipients in the arts and science.

In 1963, a meeting of the Council of Graduate Schools in the United States (CGS) on the master's degree confronted these issues. It accepted that the M.A. was losing its prestige relative to the M.B.A. and the M.F.A. and that the shortage of college teachers was so profound that only 26 percent held the doctorate, compared to 40 percent a decade earlier. Moreover, teacher certification was shaping the master's in education. Eight states required it for certification, and 11 others linked permanent certification to at least one year of full-time graduate study (CGS 1963, p. 117). A special committee on the master's degree proposed that it serve several interrelated functions: the first year of graduate study, a transitional year to make up deficiencies, and a terminal professional degree (CGS 1966).

By the 1970s, however, it became apparent that the future of the master's was in professional programs (CGS 1972, 1975, 1977). For every Ph.D. conferred in 1976, six master's degrees were awarded. In all, 1,560 new master's degrees were established and 449 terminated between 1970 and 1975 (CGS 1976). Deans and faculties sought to distinguish between professional, practitioner degrees and academic research degrees. The dichotomy between training students to satisfy professional standards for entry-level and middle-management positions and preparing them for disciplinary research and scholarship was the major consideration in determining what constituted a valid first professional degree. Colleges and universities sought to respond to the need for part-time master's degree programs, placing more emphasis on applied fields and preparation for a career, demanding fewer research requirements in practice-oriented programs, and tailoring programs to the time constraints and skill requirements of practicing professionals (CGS 1977).

A landmark study of Ph.D.s and the academic labor market distinguishes between undergraduate and graduate programs in terms of students' goals (Cartter 1976). While undergraduate education is sought primarily for enrichment and secondarily as an investment in marketable skills, "at the postbaccalaureate level, decisions to pursue advanced education are commonly job and career oriented; graduate and professional degree education are more nearly 'investment goods' in the economic analogue" (p. 73). Because of this difference in objectives, market forces affect graduate enrollments that are more responsive to expectations about career opportunities:

The student attends graduate or professional school to attain expertise in a particular field, whereas in undergraduate college the baccalaureate degree is more often the goal, and the field of study is only a secondary (and often a mid-course) consideration (p. 74).

It is difficult to project enrollments and degrees at the graduate level when conditions in the labor market affect the apparent relevance of fields of study (Cartter 1976). At the undergraduate level, students are more likely to seek generic degrees despite fluctuations in the labor market, while at the graduate level, students have less mobility across fields, and their decision to pursue a specific career is inextricably linked to their decision to enroll in a degree program. In the early 1970s, for example, a decline in employment opportunities for engineers led to a precipitous decline in enrollments. But by the end of the decade, the labor market had changed, and today a shortage of engineers exists in industry and on university faculties (Engineering Foundation 1982).

The future course of graduate education will be significantly affected by several factors, among them the growing emphasis on undergraduate education, the new value accorded to utilitarian disciplines, the decline of humanities and social sciences, the emergence of natural science and technology, and the "undesirable pattern" of federal aid's going preponderantly to science and engineering (Cartter 1976, p. 74). What Cartter did not foresee in the early 1970s was the impact of affirmative action programs on postsecondary education and, at the graduate level, on the enrollment of women in professional degree programs. While the number of degrees awarded to men in the past 10 years has been relatively stable, registering only small declines or modest growth, the number awarded to women has greatly increased: Women now earn half of all bachelor's and master's degrees, a trend expected to continue into the 1990s (Gerald 1985, p. 70).

Although conditions in the labor market continue to influence students' choices of master's programs in particular, the availability of financial aid is a key factor in postbaccalaureate enrollments (Hauptman 1986, chap. 2). From 1974 to 1984, student loans increased significantly, while service-related grants decreased sharply. Loans now constitute three-fifths of all financial assistance to master's degree students, while assistantships and fellowships represent 20 percent of their financial aid. Thus, a major policy issue is involved—"whether debt burdens and repayment obligations are influencing educational decisions, career paths, and personal choices" (p. 80).

The dividing line between academic, teaching, and research degrees has become increasingly blurred as graduate and professional schools compete for fewer potential students whose motivations and abilities differ in many respects from past generations. The issues of the 1970s revolved around the rapid expansion of higher education and state allocation of resources for graduate and professional schools. By the mid-1980s, they have shifted to discussions of proliferation, diversity, quality control, and cost. Economic and political pressures have intensified interest in the master's degree as the dominant component of postbaccalaureate education. Its development from an unearned credential at the conclusion of a young man's college education into a significant professional degree for both men and women is a distinctly American innovation in the history of higher education.

DEFINITION AND DIVERSITY

No single master's degree exists; indeed, its diversity makes it difficult to define in other than simplistic terms—that is, the first graduate degree awarded following at least one year of full-time study. And "variety in nomenclature has its counterpart in programs. Diversity makes it impossible to discuss a typical master's program. Even among professional degree programs, there is great heterogeneity" (Snell 1965, p. 87). Others define the master's degree as a "program of instruction requiring at least one, but not more than two, years of full-time equivalent academic work beyond the baccalaureate degree, the completion of which results in a master's degree conferred by the faculty and ratified by the governing board of an institution granting the degree" (Malitz 1981, p. 381) and as "the first post-baccalaureate or graduate degree, representing not less than one nor more than two years of full-time study beyond the baccalaureate. . ." (Spurr 1970, p. 14).

Nomenclature
Nowhere is the diversity of the master's degree more marked than in its nomenclature. Many master's degrees add a second designation, identifying the department or field of study—for example, Master of Science in Education or Master of Arts in Liberal Studies. The multiplicity and variety of professional programs combined with persistent efforts to differentiate them from the liberal arts and science have resulted in an avalanche of new titles. And changes in institutional types have added to the confusion. "The proliferation of professional master's degrees at institutions that formerly offered only the baccalaureate has led to an almost incomprehensible jumble of degree nomenclatures to supplement the time-honored (if loosely defined) master of arts and master of science" (Birnbaum 1983, p. 40). In 1960, Eels and Haswell identified 1,600 different degrees (and a startling 2,600 abbreviations) at 2,000 colleges and universities. At the master's level, they found some 400 varieties, including 121 different M.A. and 272 different M.S. degrees.[2]

---

2. Victorian times brought changes in nomenclature considered more appropriate for the female sex (Eels 1963, pp. 89–111; Eels and Haswell 1960, chap. 4). Mistress, Sister, Maid, or Maiden was deemed a more suitable title than Bachelor for a female graduate at the turn of the cen-

As early as the turn of the century, it had already been observed that most fairly well educated people do not know what one-fourth of the degrees mean (Thomas 1898). In 1962, the Committee on Academic Degrees of the Commission on Academic Affairs of the American Council on Education addressed problems of nomenclature (Whaley 1966), endeavoring to limit the number of master's degree titles to 50 and to standardize abbreviations, particularly in education, business, and engineering. The "chaotic situation in the titling of American academic degrees" often left students in a "maze" of confusing choices. "American higher education got along with one earned degree for 125 years after the first Bachelor of Arts was awarded by Harvard College in 1642. In the succeeding 198 years, the rate of increase has averaged about thirteen titles a year" (Whaley 1966, p. 526).

The rate of increase continues to this day as a function of new institutions, new fields of study, and increased master's level enrollments, which have more than quadrupled in the past 20 years. Peterson's guides to graduate study (Goldstein and Frary 1985, p. 989) list 667 master's degree titles coupled with 639 abbreviations. Combined degree programs created to bridge specialized fields add another 155 designations (pp. 167–75).

Curricular Models
Curricula also reflect the diversity of the master's degree, and detailed information on this topic can be obtained only from a review of graduate and professional school bulletins, some case studies on program design within a university department, comparative analyses of a particular field, and guidelines for accreditation. As in discussions about policy making, many proscriptive documents describe how to strengthen the curriculum but few its actual content.

---

tury, and some schools, particularly in the South, used one or another of those designations until 1925. In addition to Mistress of Arts, Mistress of Science, Maid of Philosophy, Maid of Science, Mistress of Philosophy, and Sister of Arts, the U.S. Commissioner of Education's annual reports listed such other neutral titles for women as Licentiate of Instruction, Laureate of Science, Proficient in Music, and Graduate in Letters (Eels 1963, p. 90). The "Mistress" series, however, including the specialized degrees, Mistress of Polite Literature and Mistress of Teaching, were the most popular.

Requirements for the master's degree are usually stated in terms of specific course credits, occasionally in terms of competencies to be achieved in meeting program goals and objectives. Its basic components vary widely in emphasis, but they generally include:

1. A common core of introductory courses appropriate to the discipline or field of study, such as foundations, theory, or research methods.
2. A concentration or specialization in a subfield of study, for example, financial accounting, rehabilitation counseling, medical-surgical nursing, or creative writing.
3. Cognate courses, often outside the department, to broaden the curriculum or to provide needed skills, such as statistics, computer programming, foreign languages, or behavioral science.
4. Integrative experience to synthesize the program's content and translate theory into practice, such as seminars, on-campus practica, internships, and other field work.
5. Summative experience to measure the student's achievement and cognitive growth by means of a thesis, research project, and/or comprehensive examination.

While the master's degree normally requires a minimum of one academic year of full-time graduate study or its equivalent in part-time work and the accumulation of not less than 30 semester hours, it requires two years of full-time graduate study and between 45 and 60 credits in most terminal degrees. Although some programs require more than two years of full-time study to complete the requirements, it generally is not the norm. Curricula are classified as academic, professional, or experiential, although some characteristics overlap. Academic degrees might be used for teaching, research, predoctoral study, or personal enrichment. Professional degrees share some of these purposes but are more likely to be oriented toward practice and terminal in nature. Experiential degrees are nontraditional in structure and design and to some extent in content and measures of achievement, although they often retain traditional requirements for credits, organization by semester, and elements of integrative and summative experiences.

Amid such diversity, comparing degrees and requirements is difficult (see table 2). Each degree may have more than one designation or title, a number of fields, subfields, or concentrations, variable requirements for credits depending on background and program objectives, and different integrative and summative experiences. The master's, moreover, may represent different degree levels. Even the familiar categorization of five degree levels—associate, bachelor's, master's, candidate/specialist/licentiate (intermediate graduate degree beyond the master's), and doctorate—is inadequate or misleading (Spurr 1970, p. 14). In addition are the first professional degrees bearing the name of doctorate but actually constituting a separate category; combined degrees at different levels (B.A./M.A.); dual or joint degrees awarded in two schools or fields simultaneously (M.A./M.B.A., J.D./M.B.A., M.P.A./M.D.), which are popular in law, medicine, business, and other professions; and master's degrees following first professional degrees in law, medicine, and dentistry, a carryover from changes in the nomenclature of those programs.

Some attention has been paid in recent years to a new theory of academic degree structures, defined as "general categorizations or curricula leading to specific academic degrees" (Spurr 1970, p. 6) and designed so as to determine the shape and structure of postsecondary education. While faculty may perceive higher education as organized into administrative units (schools, departments, research institutes), students view programs as the essence of the university. Consequently, a better conceptualization of curricula would improve the flow of students through the system (p. 6). The "ideal degree structure" would provide for a continuum of choices among colleges, programs, and curricula that would facilitate students' mobility through the system as they fulfill career objectives (p. 22).

Spurr saw the master's degree as crowning mutually exclusive discrete programs carefully delimited to a narrowly qualified student body. It is this perception that underlay his criticism of the M.A. and M.S. as the unsuccessful products of the "mere accumulation of additional credits," embodying no academic program and often

TABLE 2
REPRESENTATIVE CURRICULA

Degree	Number of Years (Full Time)	Number of Program Areas	Number of Credits	Practicum/Field Work	Exam	Thesis/Research Project
M.S.W.[a]	2	6	55–90 (0–75 required)	150 hours	X	–
M.S.N.[b]	1–2	3	36–62	2 (clinical/functional)	X	X
M.L.S.	1–2	5	36–60	120 hours (in 2-year M.L.S.)	X	X (2-year M.L.S.)
M.P.A.[c]	1–2	5	36–60	option	X	or
M.H.S.A.[d]	2	12	60	1 semester–1 year	X	or
M.F.A.[e]	2–3	6	60	72 hours	X	X
M.B.A.[f]	1–3	2	36–72	option	X	option
M.A./M.S.	1	NA	30–34	option	X	50%
M.S. Eng.[g]	1	3	32	option	X	X
M.Ed.	2	6	32–60	option	X	50%
M.A. (Journalism)[h]	1	2	32–34	option	50%	25%

Sources:
[a]Rubin 1985.
[b]NLN 1985.
[c]NASPAA 1984.
[d]Lane 1984.
[e]NASAD 1985; NAST 1983.
[f]AACSB 1984–85.
[g]ABET 1985.
[h]Peterson 1985.

awarded only as a "consolation prize." The success, he felt, of the major professional master's degrees was attributable to the fact that they met the needs of a narrowly qualified student population. His proposal for a new system of degree structures called for a reduction in the number of degree titles to allow for substantial variation in subject matter, emphasis, and quantity based on the hypothesis that "the wider the degree gates the better," the adoption of flexible time limits for the completion of degrees, the use of the master's degree to mark the completion of one phase of a student's academic career without prejudging his or her ability to embark on the next, and the compatibility of degree structures and their formal components to permit students to redirect their goals, to transfer between fields and programs, and to pursue joint degrees concurrently rather than in sequence (pp. 226–28).

This advocacy of more flexible degree structures has won few supporters. A chapter on the meaning of degrees argues that the "permutations of substance and form that are possible in graduate education constitute a great web of choices" (Storr 1973, p. 84), proposing that the master's degree stand for the completion of a program of studies beyond the undergraduate curriculum but not full competence in a mode of inquiry or field of knowledge. The standard master's degree thus should be modified to meet professional requirements.

Others deplore the lack of a common theory of curricular construction or of a general model for professional education apart from the medical school model (two years of course work and two years of clinical experience), finding it neither cogent nor relevant for the master's degree (Mayhew and Ford 1974, p. 75). Three alternative structures are proposed: (1) professional preparation programs spanning undergraduate and graduate education with some experiences in liberal arts, professional courses, and applications (skills, competencies, practica); (2) programs comprised of four components—field work, theory, foundations, and electives balanced between general and specialized studies; and (3) programs based on content, structure, and length of time to a degree (pp. 77–81). In 1977, a general matrix of the professions resembling these models was advanced (Larson 1977). It is based on a liberal education foundation followed by systematic training and testing upon which cognitive skills are progressively developed and connections made between the university and external organizations (p. 69).

The recognition that institutions would have to exercise restraint in monitoring the growth of graduate and professional programs and that external agencies and the labor market would have an effect on academic decision making has elicited many conceptualizations of the optimum master's degree framework. Much of the impetus has come from two sources, the Carnegie Commission on Higher Education (which published Spurr's, Storr's, and Mayhew and Ford's reports) and the Council of Graduate Schools (which carried on its discussion in successive annual meetings and issued periodic policy statements on the master's degree) (CGS 1966, 1976). Woven through these reports and discussions was a growing recognition that graduate education was changing in response to society's needs and students' demands and that a major part of the vigor and diversity of the master's degree was in professional programs.

Professional Degrees

What began as analogues to the classical curriculum in more vocational fields (engineering, business, nursing, education, social work, and library science) had become by 1960 the dominant mode of the professions (Berelson 1960, p. 16). Strongly supported by professional associations, private philanthropies, and university administrations, their programs had grown into autonomous schools and, through a "trickle up" process that paralleled the course of the academic master's degree, had achieved the status of postbaccalaureate study. When the professional schools made the bachelor's degree a prerequisite for entry into their programs, the master's and first professional degrees acquired even greater prestige and value. Accreditation, licensing, and economic rewards fulfilled the prophecy.

Until the 1970s, little attention was given to the role of professional schools, the nature of graduate education in the professions, and the extraordinary diversity of the master's degree in certifying professional achievement in a variety of areas (CGS 1972; Hughes 1973; Schein 1972; Spurr 1970). Although the bachelor's degree in business, education, engineering, journalism, and nursing still

What began as analogues to the classical curriculum in more vocational fields had become by 1960 the dominant mode of the professions.

accounts for the majority of degrees in those fields (Grant and Snyder 1983), it is at the master's level that the credential has gained in status and value. For better or worse, degrees are viewed as legal tender in our society, and professional degrees have greater cachet to potential employers (Hugstad 1983; NLN 1985; Ryan 1980). The bachelor's degree is perceived as an entry-level credential in business, engineering, education, and social work, but the professional master's has become a credential providing access to the ranks of middle management. Moreover, partly to meet affirmative action and equal opportunity guidelines and partly as a reflection of more formalized personnel policies, municipal governments, schools, social welfare agencies, banks, hospitals, and corporations have all devised employment criteria linked to educational background (Larson 1977). Comparative analysis of the production of M.B.A.s and first professional degrees shows similar growth curves throughout the 1970s (Stolzenberg 1985, p. 15). From 1961 to 1980, the output of first professional degrees for women jumped 2,578 percent, an average annual increase of 19 percent compounded annually.

The new prestige of the master's degree is enhanced by the ideology of the professions (Larson 1977). As credentials become more important determinants of economic success than cognitive development, training was correlated with educational achievement (p. 239), and professions served an ideological function to regulate access and justify status in the occupational order (p. xviii). The university became the center for the production of professionally relevant knowledge in which training and research depend on the same institutional structure. "As graduate and professional schools emerged at the top of the educational hierarchy, the professions acquired an institutional basis on which to develop and standardize knowledge and technologies. They also received, in university training, a powerful legitimation for their claims to cognitive and technical superiority and to social and economic benefits" (p. 136).

Initial studies criticized professional schools for being too rigid and restrictive in structure, curricula, and degree requirements (Schein 1972). By 1979, a review of research on professional education found that it had become more rigorous and less restrictive with new specializations and modes of program delivery, more part-time students, flexible graduation requirements, and intensive theoretical and practical training (Nyre and Reilly 1979, pp. 10, 16).

A study of education in medicine, law, theology, and social welfare pointed out that American professional education has a "fixed order" and that only the length of the stage varies (Hughes 1973, pp. 2–3). "It is part of the American ideology that the longer one has to go to school for a profession, the higher that profession's standing" (p. 2). Four aspects of professional education were troubling: (1) the length of schooling in the context of rising tuition, growing numbers of part-time students, and declining enrollments; (2) the degree of specialization and stratification of training and education required for higher levels of employment; (3) the access to professional study as a function of status variables favoring the graduates of elite universities and programs; and (4) the theory/practice dualism through which the student is indoctrinated into the ideology of the profession that is reinforced by the setting in which teaching and learning occur (pp. 7–15).

Other concerns about professional education appear to be even more valid in the mid-eighties (Collins 1979), particularly the tendency of the American system to delay "final professional identification" until graduate school. "As the system elaborated, the value of any particular kind and level of education came to depend less and less on any specific content that might have been learned in it, and more and more upon the sheer fact of having attained a given level and acquired the formal credential that allowed one to enter the next level" (p. 93). Furthermore, the professions and professional schools are powerfully linked, their histories firmly "intertwined" (p. 173). In a competitive environment, universities have tailored programs to meet the criteria of professional associations and accrediting agencies, allowing them to evaluate their courses, faculty, students, libraries, and administration. They have, in effect, joined forces with external bodies in deciding what constitutes a viable training program, who may gain access to it, and at what level. For example, six sources develop standards used by states to approve teacher education programs (Feistritzer 1983, p. 98): The National Council for Accreditation of Teacher Education, the National Association of State Directors of Teacher Education and Certification, regional accrediting associations, specialty organizations, state guidelines, and state law. And because most teachers graduate from state-approved programs, the standards used are more significant than individual requirements for certification.

The influence of professional associations in determining criteria for admission, educational standards, licensing, career paths, and areas of jurisdiction is such that professional schools find themselves rooted in a traditional academic model that is often rigid in structure, slow to change, narrow in specialization, and resistant to interdisciplinary structure (Schein 1972, p. 9). Law, medicine, social work, and school administration, for example, are constrained by their own associations operating under a system of status and stratification originating in their university affiliations (Larson 1977).

Despite these misgivings, the practice-oriented master's degree is more vigorous and prestigious than ever, precisely because of its close ties with the professions. Students are attracted to career programs at the graduate level. While they might elect a more general undergraduate curriculum in which the degree is more important than the discipline, the decision to seek a graduate degree is rooted in choice of career (Cartter 1976; Hugstad 1983). Indeed, the growing trend is for the master's degree to become the first professional degree, a trend that manifests itself in four different patterns: (1) Students take undergraduate and master's degrees in the same field, for example, accounting; (2) students take undergraduate work in a field related to their graduate work, for example, communications and journalism; (3) students take an undergraduate degree in a professional field followed by a substantive degree in a liberal arts discipline, for example, education followed by mathematics; or (4) students take a five- or six-year professional program yielding a combined bachelor's and master's degree, for example, engineering or architecture (Mayhew and Ford 1974, p. 56).

The decline of the research-oriented master's degree with the steady shift in enrollment from arts and science to the professions is a source of serious concern. In an effort to bridge the gap between professional and nonprofessional disciplines, one author has proposed that the three modalities of university education—undergraduate, graduate, and

professional—be related "symbiotically" on a divisional
basis through joint programs, faculty appointments, and
research (Pelikan 1983, p. 47). The interaction of the
professional schools with other divisions of the university
would acknowledge and reinforce the interdisciplinary
character of the academic enterprise and maintain the tradition of scholarship.

It may be that the new paradigm of graduate education is
the first professional degree, especially the M.B.A., J.D.,
M.D., and, although its status is not as high, the M.S. or
M.Ed. for teachers. The professional degree is the antithe-
sis of the academic degree. It is highly differentiated, and
its content and structure are based on more utilitarian and
measurable objectives, directed toward more immediate
outcomes. A new study asserts that as of 1985 more than 6
million persons held master's degrees, over 1 million had
first professional degrees, and 750,000 held earned
Ph.D.s—a total of 7 to 8 million persons with one or more
advanced degrees, only 10 percent of whom are currently
employed by colleges and universities (43 percent of all
Ph.D.s) (Bowen and Schuster 1986, p. 175). The first
professional degree reflects contemporary societal values
and is a distinctly American phenomenon. This new paradigmatic shift has further bifurcated graduate education,
and the issue is not the devaluation of the baccalaureate or
the Master of Arts: It is the new dominance of professionalism at all levels, associate through doctoral degree.

THE ASSESSMENT OF QUALITY

The past two decades have witnessed an ongoing dialogue over how quality should be assessed. In graduate and professional education, this process has tended to focus on the doctorate in prestigious research universities (Cartter 1966; Jones, Lindzey, and Coggeshall 1982; Roose and Anderson 1970) and to a lesser extent on reputational rankings of prominent professional schools (Blau and Margulies 1973; Cartter and Solmon 1977). Some attention has also been given to developing indices of quality at the undergraduate level (Kuh 1981). The historical development of quality assessment is traced in comprehensive reviews of the literature (Conrad and Blackburn 1985b; Lawrence and Green 1980); Webster 1985). At the institutional level, the role of accreditation in quality assessment has been discussed (Harcleroad 1980; Millard 1984; Young et al. 1983) and efforts to develop quality criteria undertaken by the Council of Graduate Schools in cooperation with the Graduate Record Examination Board (GREB)(CGS 1976, 1979, 1982b), by regional accrediting associations (Kirkwood 1985), and by state coordinating boards (Smartt 1984).

Until recently, little emphasis has been placed on assessing the quality of the master's degree. In addressing this issue, it has been recognized that neither reputational rankings nor quantitative assessments of prepackaged variables are adequate for this level of degree (Conrad and Blackburn 1985a; CGS 1979; Webster 1979). Rather, the focus has been on identifying multidimensional indicators that emerge from the research rather than being imposed on programs a priori (Conrad and Blackburn 1985a).

An assessment of departmental quality in regional colleges and universities investigated 45 departments in 14 institutions (Conrad and Blackburn 1985a). Using departmental quality rather than reputational ratings as the dependent variable, it identified 73 independent variables in four categories (faculty, students, programs, facilities) (p. 283), which were reduced to 32 variables to determine the degree of their correlation with departmental quality (p. 288). The study concluded that "multiple and diverse factors contribute to graduate departmental excellence" and that those factors are "more multidimensional in regional colleges and universities than in leading research universities" (p. 293). In terms of the master's degree, the study found little correlation between departmental quality and graduate degrees awarded or number and range of degree programs and moderate correlation with the proportion of degree programs at the advanced graduate level, suggesting "qualitative dimensions seldom explored in previous research" (p. 292).

The need for multidimensional indicators of quality is even more critical in assessments of professional education. The use of reputational peer ratings of professional schools has two problems: (1) The same professional schools are consistently identified in the ratings; and (2) the diversity of professional schools necessitates the use of different criteria than in academic disciplines that are usually assessed on a departmental basis (Lawrence and Green 1980, p. 31). A survey of deans and directors of undergraduate business schools and M.B.A. programs and of senior personnel executives found that faculty reputations were the "overwhelming factor in ratings" of the best business schools (Hunger and Wheelen 1980a). One weakness with this approach is apparent in the results of this survey, however: Personnel executives ranked five exclusively *graduate* business schools among the top 10 *undergraduate* schools as well (p. 26). Thus, "neither quantitative nor qualitative methods of assessment alone are satisfactory for adequately and accurately estimating quality," but a "holistic perspective on quality assessment" is most useful (Kuh 1981, p. 31).

Accreditation has focused on two concerns—educational quality and institutional integrity. According to the Council on Postsecondary Accreditation, 16 specialized units and six regional accrediting associations are concerned with master's level programs (COPA 1984). The regional associations are supported by institutional dues from 2,800 member institutions and provide the basic framework for accreditation. Both accreditation and mandated standards affect the design of programs and the process through which colleges and universities monitor the quality of programs. Although the meaning of the college degree should reflect more accurately the knowledge, skills, and personal qualities it certifies through its award, the degree no longer signifies comparability in educational outcomes (Young et al. 1983, p. 400). This factor has implications for its value, particularly as accreditation is a voluntary process, depending on self-regulation and informal monitoring.

COPA's role has been to discourage proliferation and specialization, to evaluate educational quality, and to measure educational outcomes (Harcleroad 1980, p. 29). Its current director defines quality at the graduate level in terms of special program objectives, whether programs are research oriented, disciplinary or interdisciplinary, oriented toward beginning a career or developing one's skills, or a combination (Millard 1984, p. 41). But the proliferation of institutions categorized as "postsecondary" following passage of the Education Amendments of 1972 might have exacerbated "the perennial degree-mill problem" (Harcleroad 1980, p. 34). As the range of postsecondary institutions grew, the proclivity increased for offering more master's degrees, cheapening them in the degree hierarchy and accelerating the schism between research and professional degrees. Nontraditional efforts at diversity—distance learning, external degrees, off-campus programs—have made quality control more difficult to manage (Dressel 1978; Harcleroad 1980, p. 35). While coordination of self-studies and program reviews has improved the function of quality control, the plethora of agencies and commissions with overlapping jurisdiction in accreditation of degree programs has been somewhat problematic, partly because of the varying expectations and levels of authority of accrediting agencies in relation to national and state boards, partly because of the effectiveness of self-regulation, and partly because of the feasibility of applying comparable criteria to disparate programs and institutions.

Recognition is growing that quantifiable data are not adequate to measure academic quality.

Quality is an elusive concept, and no matter what criteria are applied by external arbiters, it is the institution that determines the nature, content, and quality of its programs through the resources it allocates and the faculty it hires. Recognition is growing that quantifiable data are not adequate to measure academic quality. One major issue is whether different evaluative criteria should be used to assess the quality of master's programs and doctoral programs, professional degrees and research degrees. A variety of criteria would be needed to assess the productivity of faculty research, teaching, advisement, student outcomes, facilities, resources that are specific to a department, and the complex relationship of programs to the surrounding community (Webster 1979). Reputational rankings should rely not on a single measure of faculty output but on multidimensional considerations more germane to the program's objectives and students' needs (Webster 1979). In this connection, the Ohio Board of Regents in its most recent master plan (1982, p. 18) endorsed the position that the diversity of objectives in practitioner master's programs implied diverse measures of excellence and precluded a single set of universally accepted criteria of quality. Ohio colleges and universities were directed to define the purposes and expectations of their programs and to develop their own statements of acceptable quality (p. 18).

The CGS Task Force on Quality
In 1973, the Council of Graduate Schools (CGS) and the Graduate Record Examination Board formed a steering committee to identify "dimensions of quality" in doctoral programs and to survey the opinions of 60 graduate deans of arts and science on the topic (Downey 1979, p. 86). The Educational Testing Service (ETS) undertook a two-year study for CGS of multidimensional aspects of quality in doctoral programs; the Dimensions of Quality in Doctoral Education project grew out of concern about the limitations of the highly publicized and controversial reputational studies of the American Council on Education (ACE). Thirty program characteristics were field tested in three disciplines—chemistry, psychology, and history—in 25 universities, and the results were disseminated in a detailed technical report (Clark, Hartnett, and Baird 1976). In its summary of the research results, CGS emphasized the potential of self-study and the use of multidimensional frameworks in assessing quality (Clark and Hartnett 1977).

In its revised statement on the master's degree, CGS (1976, p. 7) had emphasized the role of vigorous institutional reviews in assessing program quality and voluntary termination of substandard programs, obviating the need for external evaluation. The devaluation of degrees was becoming a major issue, variously attributed to the expansion of knowledge and the expansion of degrees, to poor preparation of incoming students, and to the nature of the licensing function (CGS 1977). The climate was one of assessment and retrenchment.

In 1978, CGS established the Task Force on the Assessment of Master's Level Programs to explore the applicability of doctoral criteria for evaluating academic and professional master's degree programs and to adapt the Dimensions of Quality in Doctoral Education at the master's level (Downey 1979, p. 86). The questionnaire addressed two issues: (1) What dimensions of the program are important for the assessment of quality? and (2) what procedures and methods should be used to conduct the assessment? It hypothesized at the outset that quality in a master's program can be measured in six areas: faculty, students, resources, learning environment, programs, and alumni. Several characteristics for determining quality were listed for each area and specific indicators and sources provided for each characteristic.

The task force constructed a survey instrument to gather data on what characteristics and indicators would be most useful in evaluating both academic and professional/technical master's degrees. A survey of graduate deans elicited a 56 percent response (202 responses) concerning important program elements in the master's program review. The final report, issued in January 1979, was presented at a conference at the University of Maryland (CGS 1979). The task force worked with ETS to design and field test questionnaires that would enable graduate departments to assess the quality of their master's programs. Separate versions were developed, based on seven criteria (quality of faculty, quality of students, institutional resources, learning environment, academic offerings, degree requirements, and characteristics of alumni) for different types of institutions, departments, and program areas. In 1981, CGS, the Association of Graduate Schools, and the Graduate Record Examination Board set up a new Graduate Program Self-Assessment Service (GPSA). Three sets of questionnaires were designed for use by universities to be administered to faculty, students, and alumni of the department or school being evaluated. Sixteen composite indicators of characteristics of the master's program were used, ranging from scholarly excellence to student outcomes. In three years of operation, the service has processed 10,000 to 20,000 questionnaires each year, representing 80 to 100 programs in 30 to 40 institutions. (Reports of a comparative data analysis in humanities, social science, and physical science were scheduled for publication in late 1986.)

A series of papers at the Maryland conference raised several other significant issues about quality assessment of the master's degree:

1. The American degree structure distinguishes between levels based on academic achievement and the nature and type of study. While most professions have both basic and advanced undergraduate and graduate programs, liberal arts graduates enrolling for professional master's degrees often lack the required foundation, necessitating a two-tiered or restructured basic program and additional credit hours for those with no background in the discipline (CGS 1979).
2. Confusion in objectives of master's programs may stem from attempts to provide general education, prepare doctoral candidates, and provide quasi-vocational guidance. By the same token, the master's degree as a "useful credential" implies measuring outcomes through career goals, employment, and self-fulfillment (p. 48).
3. The lack of consensus on whether professional preparation should be postbaccalaureate is linked to the widespread practice of offering undergraduate courses for graduate credit, blurring the lines between basic and advanced courses of study.
4. Nontraditional degree programs pose special problems of standards, accountability, and alternative delivery systems. Multidimensional programs may warrant qualitative and quantitative measures of effectiveness (p. 39).
5. The organizing principle of dual degrees is to increase multiple competencies of practitioners at the advanced professional level and to eliminate duplication of course requirements (p. 23). Dual degrees facilitate the acquisition of two professional credentials in a shorter time and at a lower cost.
6. Distinctions in evaluation criteria may be appropriate to distinguish between professional and academic programs, particularly when the former is linked more directly to employers, many of whom teach in professional schools, sit on university boards of trustees, serve as employment recruiters, and control professional associations and journals (p. 69).

The State and Quality Assessment
Assessing quality in the master's degree involves two kinds of problems: (1) the large and diverse population of pro-

grams whose content, structure, and objectives vary considerably among program types and institutional varieties; and (2) the responsibility to educate and train new clienteles across disciplines through new arrangements of curriculum and systems of delivery (Pelczar and Frances 1984, p. 5). The states lack a clear conception of graduate education: "Collectively, the states' educational policies do not constitute a national perspective or policy on graduate education" (p. 9). This observation is confirmed by a review of state master plans, which vary considerably in their specific requirements. States are now more concerned with accountability, and several have instituted performance audits, management by objectives, program evaluations, and increased regulation (Young et al. 1983, p. 73). A major liability of this strategy is to "shift the focus from access for all groups in society to maintenance of elite quality standards" (Eyler 1984, p. 63).

Official perceptions of the master's degree sometimes reinforce the lower status of the Master of Arts. Florida's master plan acknowledges that students who fail to achieve candidacy for the doctorate "are led to settle for the lesser master's degree" (Florida State Board of Education 1982, p. 33). Several states have adopted regulations to discourage duplication of master's degree programs, particularly in state-operated institutions. At the same time, they often encourage degrees that are specialized, distinctive, and diverse. Indeed, in Florida, "master's degree programs may be duplicated in different areas of the state when the advantages of duplication significantly outweigh the increased costs" (p. 32). These policies may have the unintended consequence of encouraging the proliferation of degree designations in an effort to be distinctive enough to mount new master's programs. Joint degree programs, nontraditional delivery systems through off-campus courses, distance learning, and other mechanisms impose new burdens, constraints, and demands on what accreditation agencies are able to accomplish in quality assessment (Young et al. 1983, p. 74).

A content analysis of research on graduate and professional education identified five issues that dominate in studies and analyses of government regulation and policy (Wild, Fortna, and Knapp 1978, p. 57): (1) the rationale for establishing state regulation; (2) the scope of regulatory agencies' enforcement powers; (3) state policies for private and public higher education; (4) the kinds of information required by state and federal agencies; and (5) the mechanisms for statewide planning. One concern was how to maintain quality programs in the context of changing social and manpower trends, the relationship of the university and the job market, and the emphasis on economic return rather than intellectual achievement as a major outcome of graduate education (p. 70).

In 1969, New York became the first state to propose standards of quality for master's programs. The State Education Department's Divisions of Teacher Education and of Academic Program Review focused on the master's degree to identify those factors that affect quality (CGS 1979, p. 75). Of the 2,100 master's programs, curricula were reviewed in 56 of 82 institutions—238 in education, 235 in liberal arts, 98 in professional fields, and 29 in theology (p. 76). As a result, a moratorium was declared on the development of new doctoral programs, a commission on doctoral education was appointed, and new regulations were adopted for registration in graduate and professional degree program that emphasized needs assessments, student outcomes, and evaluation criteria (Bureau of College Evaluation 1972).

New York found that the growth of the master's degree had been rapid, unplanned, and uncontrolled in the sixties. Programs were administered with little appraisal or review, admissions criteria were too elastic, curricula varied widely in quality, and large numbers of nonmatriculated and part-time students were enrolled. In many programs, students could accumulate credits with no systematic training in research, no thesis, or no comprehensive examination. The main objective was permanent certification, but academic advisement was weak, faculty were often unqualified, and programs showed little innovation or responsiveness to new social or professional needs (Bureau of College Evaluation 1972). In half of the institutions surveyed, one or more programs (over two-thirds of the 600 total) had deficient curricula. Beginning in 1969, the state gave institutional aid to private colleges and universities in accordance with the Bundy formula granting aid for degrees awarded, an added incentive to offer master's degrees. Throughout the 1970s, master's degrees were reviewed that were part of doctoral programs. Since 1979, the state has conducted periodic reviews to measure the effect of its activities in assessing academic programs, and in 1985–86, it initiated the second cycle of formal master's reviews in 100 elementary and bilingual education programs in public and private colleges and universities, using measures of quantitative productivity, institutional self-studies, out-of-state consultants, and site visits.

Other states have adopted this model, although only New York monitors graduate programs in both public and private institutions. Systemwide or segmental program reviews in other states have tended to focus on master's degrees as part of the doctorate or in teacher education. In most states, however, program review is limited to new programs in state universities and colleges, and it is characterized by a high level of generality in the decision-making process. The major dimensions of state and institutional response to improved quality are analyzed in a series of papers linking the process to financial incentives and to a new emphasis on excellence in education spurred by the slowdown in the national economic growth, the decline in the college-age population and in the expansion of most age groups, and the decline in students' academic performance (Folger 1984, p. 1).

Fiscal policies in the past two decades have promoted growth through appropriations for new programs, through new institutions, and through tuition subsidies that gave colleges "a margin of extra resources" (Folger 1984, p. 2). The issue now confronting these institutions is how to improve standards in a period of reduced resources. The renewed interest in quality has two possible outcomes: insistence on clear goals and expectations for performance and more accountability for results (p. 3). An examination of the definitions of quality and different priorities for improvement found that "the end of growth and the achievement of broad access to higher education, combined with concern about economic stagnation and lack of confidence in particular, have led to an emphasis by policy makers on accountability and program effectiveness in higher education" (Eyler 1984, p. 71). The result is a "proliferation of state initiatives" that includes higher admission standards, incentive aid, and targeted special funding. And the extent to which such initiatives can be implemented and sustained politically over time is the critical issue of the 1980s (p. 71).

State education agencies are using program reviews for a variety of purposes. Academic program reviews involve three categories of state/institutional relationships: (1) an indirect coordinating role, primarily related to the collection of data about enrollments and degrees and resulting in statewide program inventories; (2) periodic assessments (either institutional or staff-conducted) as a means of enhancing existing programs and developing new ones; and (3) direct involvement in reviews by out-of-state consultants, leading to termination and consolidation of programs and increased categorical funding (Smartt 1984, p. 44). Universities with a concentration of graduate programs have used program review for allocating internal resources. Further, reallocations of resources are usually determined at the institutional (school or departmental) level rather than at the state level and are more likely to occur as a result of qualitative than of quantitative reviews. And the reallocation of resources is actually a "more significant outcome" than cost savings, which are commonly a by-product of "fiscal exigency" (pp. 46–49). In North Carolina, for example, program reviews were used as an incentive to improve quality, and reviews of professional programs were conducted in the health professions, home economics, teacher education, and engineering, with others planned in business and management, computer science, communications, and foreign language (p. 51). Between 1977 and 1981, those reviews led to the discontinuance of 63 teacher education programs deemed unsatisfactory and the redirection of faculty to engineering and the sciences (p. 54).

External agencies, state governing boards, and institutional officials are now involved in quality control. Professional associations of graduate schools are also designing criteria and procedures for periodic evaluation and approval of new programs. Increased attention is being given the master's degree, particularly in professional schools. We can anticipate more emphasis on self-regulation as dependence on external resources and technological changes give new impetus to a major restructuring of the educational delivery system.

MAJOR PROFESSIONAL DEGREES

Business and Management

The business school did not emerge full-blown in the 1960s
and 1970s. It evolved from a liberal arts–oriented model at
the turn of the century. Under the leadership of President
Charles Eliot, Harvard in 1908 became the first university
to offer the M.B.A. It established an independent business
school in 1913, and as more freestanding schools were
formed by state and private universities, pressures
mounted to differentiate between undergraduate schools
of commerce and the graduate business school that was
drawn inexorably into the orbit of business and industry. It
was not until 1958 that the American Assembly of Collegiate Schools of Business (AACSB) began to set minimum
accreditation standards for graduate schools.

A highly influential report published at the close of the
1950s under the sponsorship of the Carnegie Corporation
sounded the opening salvos for professionalizing business
education (Gordon and Howell 1959). It recommended that
graduate schools jettison the arts and science model, estab-
lish more rigorous requirements for entrance and award of
degrees, and adopt a two-year M.B.A. with two tracks,
one for students with an undergraduate concentration in
business and another for those without it (p. 286). That
model rapidly became the norm, replacing the one-year
master's program for undergraduate business majors that
had prevailed from the inception of graduate business education. The Carnegie report also envisioned the M.B.A. as
a teaching and research degree for those who aspired to
teaching positions at undergraduate colleges or as the
equivalent of an M.A. or M.S. in a social science discipline
(p. 286). Subsequently, the AACSB denominated three
types of M.B.A. programs: (1) type A to provide basic
business knowledge as a foundation for career development; (2) type B to provide theoretical knowledge and specialized instruction for careers in management; and (3) type
C to provide broader and more advanced training for a
spectrum of professional careers.

In the 1960s, graduate schools greatly expanded their
faculty to provide training in cognate disciplines like mathematics, psychology, and engineering and to introduce new
concentrations in finance, marketing, production, and
advanced management (Hugstad 1983, p. 41). Business
schools introduced more specializations to position them-

selves for the "new vocationalism of the 1970s" (p. 42). By 1982–83, business and management concentrations were reported in 45 specialties ranging from insurance, investments, personnel, and real estate to trade, marketing, tourism, and hotel/motel management (OERI 1985, pp. 46–49). Highly specialized concentrations appear to have been particularly pervasive in second- and third-tier programs as business schools sought to respond to the needs of corporate employers.

Enrollments soared in the 1960s and 1970s, and business schools were one of the few divisions of higher education left unscathed by student protests and demands for relevance (Hugstad 1983, p. 42). Their ability to generate income, attract support from business and industry, and enhance the image of universities gave them greater status within the academic community. And the production of M.B.A.s grew exponentially (Stolzenberg 1985, pp. 11–12). Between 1962 and 1972, the number of degrees conferred increased tenfold—and continued upward into the 1980s. By 1982, one out of every five degrees awarded was an M.B.A. Its programs grew from 285 in 1970 to 608 in 1984, a 113 percent increase. By 1981, business schools accounted for 22 percent of all undergraduate and graduate students (Ouchi 1985, p. 11). Women were responsible for a significant portion of the growth rate—11 percent of all M.B.A. enrollments and 17.6 percent of all M.B.A. degrees conferred in 1982, a figure "high enough to double annual master's degree production by women every 4.3 years" (Stolzenberg 1985, p. 13).

The theory-practice nexus
The theme of several recent studies of the M.B.A. has been the dichotomy between the training received in business schools and the needs of corporations for professionals able to employ new technologies. The major issues are theory versus practice, specialization versus general training, quality versus quantity, criteria for admission, goals and purposes, emphases of the program, and methods of instruction and delivery. A special report of the Carnegie Foundation that analyzes education and training in the corporate sector stands in stark contrast to Gordon and Howell's 1959 study of business education (Eurich 1985). Of 18 "corporate colleges with academic degrees" subsumed

into three groups of sponsors (corporations, industry groups, and professional/research/consulting organizations) 11 offer master's degrees, and together they provide a total of 24 master's degrees that differ radically from the older, institutionalized M.B.A. (pp. 85–122).

These degrees range from the Master of Software Engineering at the Wang Institute of Graduate Studies in Massachusetts to the Master of Manufacturing Management at the General Motors Institute of Engineering and Management in Michigan (table 3, pp. 89–95). The most innovative is National Technological University, an organization specializing in distance learning sponsored by a consortium of corporations, federal agencies, and the Association for Media-based Continuing Education for Engineers, which offers an external degree in five engineering fields for completion of courses via satellite. Open admissions policies permit all qualified persons outside the sponsoring corporation to enroll. Innovative methods are used—distance learning, videotapes, individualized programs for professionals, and closed-circuit interactive telecommunications. These institutions "decided to add the graduate degree programs because of a perceived need. . . . It is the age-old problem of the integration of theory and practice, of the application of knowledge and training, the combination of conceptual study and actual work" (Eurich 1985, p. 121).

Thus, corporate education has become a "booming industry" at a time when higher education is being admonished to raise standards, strengthen admissions and graduation requirements, and disband unproductive programs. The Carnegie report underscores the economic bind in which higher education finds itself. A combination of state and federal mandates, fiscal constraints, and public/private competition for students and resources had eroded the quality of programs through steady assaults on operating budgets, endowments, and grants. At the same time, costly technologies have the potential for changing teaching and learning: Corporations can experiment with new technologies while universities lack the resources to build expensive training facilities or to equip existing classrooms with sophisticated hardware that might have to be upgraded frequently. Higher education cannot compete with corporations, neither in recruiting training personnel from the upper echelons of business, industry, and academe, nor in

Corporations can experiment with new technologies while universities lack the resources to build expensive training facilities or to equip existing classrooms....

building strategically located training centers for tailor-made programs. Few if any colleges can package their offerings as attractively, as cost effectively, or as business specifically as corporations. And the question is whether they should use their resources to compete with corporate education. Businesses spend an estimated $40 to 60 billion a year on in-house and company-sponsored education—an amount roughly equivalent to that spent on all higher education in 1981–82 (Eurich 1985, p. 6). The trend from college to corporate classrooms is of concern to educators and state policy makers, and giving approval to a double standard for quality control in postsecondary education—one for colleges and universities and another for noncollegiate institutions—is a distinct danger. Who, if anyone, will monitor corporate degree programs?

Alternative degree models

The master's degree programs at the Arthur D. Little Management Education Institute and at Wang, both of which are accredited by the New England Association of Schools and Colleges, seek to provide advanced training for middle- and senior-level managers (Spruell 1985). The Little Institute was founded in 1965 at the request of the U.S. Agency for International Development to create new managers for developing nations. It offers an 11-month master's program in international management. To date, 860 students from 57 countries (20 percent Asian) have been granted this degree.

While the M.B.A. is the most popular graduate business degree, some universities offer two-year M.S. degrees that are similar in scope and emphasis. Among them are the Master of Science in Management (M.S.M.) awarded by MIT and Purdue, the Master of Science in Industrial Management (M.S.I.M.) offered by Carnegie-Mellon, the Master of Management (M.M.) offered by Northwestern and the University of Michigan at Dearborn, and various M.S. degrees in specializations like accounting, quantitative analysis, operations research, finance, real estate, and insurance. An M.S. in Business Policy is designed to offer executives the opportunity to upgrade their management skills without interrupting their careers. At the Columbia Business School, each class goes through the program as an integrated group, taking required and elective courses for a total of 36 credits. Classes meet on Fridays from 8:30 a.m. to 6:30 p.m. for four academic terms, each of which starts with a one-week, full-time program in residence at a conference center. In addition, 125 universities offer a joint M.B.A./J.D. degree, 36 a joint M.B.A./engineering degree, and 86 a joint M.B.A. with a degree in fields like health, public administration, and education.

The School of Business at Southern Methodist University has developed an experimental one-year M.B.A. as an "action management" program emphasizing field-based projects in business and nonprofit organizations in the local community (Wolfe and Byrne 1980). The rationale is that knowledge can be acquired and skills developed simultaneously with project-based experience. "Action management" students complete two-thirds of their M.B.A. program in experiential learning, exercising greater personal initiative, depending less on faculty for their learning, and having multiple opportunities to fill managerial roles. Such an approach is valid in graduate business education.

Professional schools have been criticized generally for being too rigid and restrictive in their program structure and content and in their criteria for admissions and degrees (Schein 1972), but the dilemma between theory and practice has intensified in today's competitive environment. The issue in experiential professional learning is whether change and innovation are possible within the hierarchical structure of the educational system, whether the dominant model of block program scheduling permits an adequate response to individual students' interests, abilities, and needs, or whether students must conform to requirements for a degree designed by faculty, endorsed by accrediting and licensing agencies, and reified by tradition into established policies and dogma. Criteria for qualitative evaluation of programs tend to formalize structure, processes, and outcomes. It is far easier to measure uniform quantitative variables than to individualize each student's program commensurate with his or her needs. What we have to be wary of, however, is the designer degree shaped to the needs of the wearer and apt to be high fashion rather than of classic cut (CGS 1975, p. 138).

A study conducted in the 1970s comparing the perceptions of four groups—liberal arts and business school deans, university placement directors, and corporate executives—on the relative emphasis that universities should give to career training vis-à-vis the liberal arts found significant variations in the groups' expectations concerning the appropriate educational training for business careers and the optimum outcomes of business education (Hugstad 1983, p. 89). Corporate personnel considered science and engineering backgrounds more desirable than either business or liberal arts and career preparation to be a cardinal objective, while academic deans (business and liberal arts) did not view career preparation and training as central to their mission (p. 75).

A survey of deans and faculty of business schools, 1978 alumni of M.B.A. programs, and Fortune 500 executives found a wide divergence of views on the degree itself (Jenkins, Reizenstein, and Rodgers 1984). The participants disagreed about the goals of a quality program, the relevance of curricula, career development skills, and the utility of the degree for top management positions (p. 21). The major issues were dichotomies between generalist and specialist or breadth versus depth. Most M.B.A. programs require foundations courses, specialization, and generalized training. Executives preferred more applied approaches and demonstrated little regard for admissions criteria based on GMAT scores, while most M.B.A. programs use such scores in combination with cumulative grade point averages as twin predictors of academic success. Executives advocated that more weight be placed on the applicant's ability to perform in and out of school than on test-taking skills (p. 30). Thus, a "compelling argument [could be made] for reevaluating and perhaps restructuring graduate business schools' curricula" (p. 30). In another study, executives favored training for short-term operational problem solving, while academics emphasized long-range "strategic" planning (Rehder 1982, p. 64). Business schools, the author charged, had sacrificed educational quality to rapid expansion and growth with the result that they had become "a mass education cafeteria where unappetizing functional course credit hours are thrown on the student's plate. The diet may be filling but certainly not nourishing to the intellect or the soul" (p. 68). Integrating advanced technical training into a broad universe of experience and learning is one way to approach the problem, and if business schools fail to adapt, corporations may assume their functions to an even greater degree (p. 11). Others, however, wonder whether business schools are awarding vocational diplomas or academic degrees and urge them to move away from highly specialized programs into the development of generalists with broader societal views (Kiechel 1979, p. 50).

Several factors contribute to the success of the M.B.A. A survey of graduate students at the University of Illinois found that their chief objective was a terminal master's degree, like the M.B.A., that conferred full professional status. After all, "the critical aspect of academic success is the earning of degrees" (Berg and Ferber 1983, p. 639), and the thrust of business education is to elevate the M.B.A. to the level of a first professional degree comparable to law and medicine. A large undergraduate base and greater coherence between graduate and undergraduate programs, particularly with respect to the introduction of computer technology and stricter quantitative requirements, have also contributed to its growth (Hennessey 1984, p. 23). In addition, one-year M.B.A.s like Southern Methodist University's action management program or exclusionary proposals like that of the American Institute of Certified Public Accountants for state legislation mandating a fifth-year master's to enter the field of public accounting may further accelerate M.B.A. enrollments. Although the AACSB opposes the requirement, Florida and Hawaii have already instituted it (AACSB 1986). Moreover, employment opportunities and starting salaries for new M.B.A.s attract graduate students seeking "the highest rate of return" rather than "the intellectual content" of its programs (Stolzenberg 1985, p. 24).

While the demand for undergraduate and graduate business education will persist into the 1990s, the continuing success of the M.B.A. is far from assured. Very little has been done to control its proliferation owing to the generous accrediting policies of the AACSB (Schmotter 1984, p. 13). It remains to be seen whether the M.B.A. will retain its marketability when it becomes less of a status symbol in hiring. As has been demonstrated in teacher education, a credential certifying to professional competence loses its prestige in direct proportion to the numbers who hold it, a phenomenon that leads to further differentiation at higher degree levels. Monitoring is perfunctory at best in most states, and academic standards vary greatly. South Carolina, for example, encourages public institutions offering business degrees to seek AACSB accreditation or to otherwise meet AACSB standards. In the New York metropolitan area, course credit requirements for 15 M.B.A. programs range from 36 to 72, depending on the undergraduate major (Azzara 1985). The typical program consists of a required core of 12 to 30 credits and a concentration of required and elective courses. Fairleigh Dickinson University offers no fewer than 17 concentrations, from Accounting for Non-Accountants to Pharmaceutical Chemical Studies. Quality control and diversity of programs are among the most serious issues confronting the profession (Nanus 1984, p. 15), but the M.B.A. curriculum also needs to address issues of productivity, international business, the transfer of technology, information systems, and entrepreneurship (Schmotter 1984, p. 12).

The shift of management's education to the corporate sector can have serious consequences (Eurich 1985). Much of the future of business education will depend on its ability to recover a sizable share of this market, "designing education for emerging new fields and professions" and attracting talented M.B.A.s to seek teaching careers in its business schools (p. 122). One trend is for education to study management as it affects the public sector. Thus, Yale's innovative School of Organization and Management focuses on the political, regulatory, and international environment. Yet another trend is cooperative programs between universities and industry (CGS/NSF 1980). "More and better bridges [are necessary] . . . between the academy and business" regarding the roles of business education (Hugstad 1983, p. 119). Yet the university has a social responsibility, and joint industrial/university research has ethical implications, involving issues of autonomy, resources, and the mission of the university (Bok 1982). It seems clear that as enrollments in graduate business begin to stabilize at current levels and the need for new M.B.A.s diminishes, the debate will heighten as to current policies and future directions.

Teacher Education
Major problems in education concern the effect of public policy on teacher training programs. Certification and

licensing requirements have a major impact on graduate schools of education (GSEs), particularly because almost one-third of all master's degrees are in education. Historically, however, the teaching degree does not have the status of the M.B.A., its closest rival, for reasons that are embedded in its history and in the nature of American society. Originally, the M.A. and M.S. in education were the preferred credentials for those seeking positions as secondary school teachers and administrators. Later, the master's was recommended as a degree for community college and lower division college teachers or as the midpoint degree for the Doctor of Education and the Doctor of Arts.

Harvard College established the first seminary for teachers in 1831 and began offering the earned master's degree in the field about 40 years later. In 1922, Harvard was also the first university to offer the Ed.D. as an applied doctorate, partly to bypass more stringent Ph.D. requirements in foreign languages. In school administration, the aspiring superintendent was admonished to obtain a doctorate to differentiate his status from the teacher, who was generally female and, at least in elementary education, needed only a high school diploma and two years of normal school. A study of 623 small liberal arts colleges found that by 1962 one-fifth of them had master's programs, mainly in education (Ness and James 1962). Many of these programs originated as a response to the postwar demand for teachers, and those who attended were likely to live or work near the respective college, 25 percent of which were affiliated with a church.

In the more prestigious research universities, graduate schools of education are more concerned with doctoral research and scholarship than with master's level teacher training (Judge 1982). Graduate schools can be divided into three categories: (1) the arts and science model that nurtures Ph.D.s with foundation- and government-sponsored research; (2) the dominant professional schools of medicine, law, and business in which degrees from "the right schools earn advancement, prestige, and money"; and (3) the graduate schools of education, whose identity in "the higher education galaxy" is less certain. Distancing themselves from their credentialing roles, they are viewed as neither arts and science nor professional schools and are dismissed as irrelevant and remote.

GSEs are distinguished from other professional schools in the reasons for attending them: to acquire a needed credential, to secure renewal or extension of a license, and to advance incrementally on the salary scale. Students are employed older women and minorities, attend part time, and are apt to differ in abilities, backgrounds, and academic needs from the traditional postbaccalaureate, full-time student. Many acquire master's degrees and sixth-year certificates to move from the classroom to the principal's office. "The GSE serves as an escalator by which one climbs from the ranks of teaching to other, superior, or more attractive occupations" (Judge 1982, p. 38). GSEs stress the "G," concentrating their resources on doctoral programs and aligning their standards (but not their purposes) with graduate schools of arts and science, especially in the social sciences. Requirements for admission to master's programs are lower, courses are often fragmented, understaffed, repetitive, or incoherent, and students often enroll in them to fulfill requirements for certification or promotion. Thus, a "pervasive contradiction . . . lies . . . at the heart of graduate schools of education" (p. 43).

Society's view of education places the teaching profession below medicine and law, which are perceived as sharing greater financial and professional status, and the lack of a clear mission among GSEs helps perpetuate the low relative value of the master's degree in education (Judge 1982). "Little prestige attaches to the role of teacher and little to his or her education and training," which are seen as by-products of a liberal arts education (p. 46). As long as teaching remains at the base of the professional pyramid, its status will likely continue to be low. By providing upwardly mobile routes away from teaching (out of the classroom), GSEs implement a "latitudinarian policy" with a bewildering array of choices based on a negative unifying principle. Responding to narrower academic imperatives, they abandon their base without finding an alternative one. In short, schools of education are in low repute on their campuses, lack a central focus because they are defined by the academic disciplines rather than their impact on the profession, and are dominated by a few prestigious graduate schools.

This "undifferentiated view of schools of education" has been criticized, based on three major historical developments that shaped teacher education: (1) the evolution of teachers colleges into liberal arts colleges or as units of comprehensive universities in which teacher education was "submerged"; (2) the rise of the land-grant university, in which education was assigned a low priority in relation to other practical subjects; and (3) the attitude of the major private universities toward teacher education as a way of "ameliorating societal ills" (Atkin 1983, p. 66). These models of professional education are distinct from the single-model medical or law school and more analogous to business schools characterized by divergent histories and objectives (p. 67).

Several proposals have been made in the past 25 years to combine a four-year liberal undergraduate education with a two-year professional master's that culminates in a full-time teaching internship. The Master of Arts in Teaching (M.A.T.), initiated at Harvard and other prestigious universities in the 1960s, was designed as a 4-1 program in which intensive course work was combined with a teaching internship as the major graduate experience. This model has now been adapted further by a group of prestigious research-oriented GSEs seeking to eliminate preservice teacher preparation for undergraduates and to make the master's degree more "professional." Under the leadership of Judith Lanier of Michigan State University, the Holmes Group proposes a differentiated structure of three levels of teacher preparation: Instructor, Professional Teacher, and Career Professional, creating career incentives "to improve the quality, engagement, and commitment of the teaching force" (Holmes Group 1986, p. 36).

In short, schools of education are in low repute on their campuses, lack a central focus . . . and are dominated by a few prestigious graduate schools.

In the 1960s, the Ford Foundation spent $29 million on "Breakthrough Programs" designed to improve teacher training (Coley and Thorpe 1986, p. 20). Forty-three institutions of higher education participated in the programs, although the majority of the recipients were selective liberal arts institutions in the northeast. Programs ranged from a five-year undergraduate degree and a combined bachelor's and master's degree to an M.A.T. for liberal arts baccalaureates seeking careers as secondary school teachers. The 4-2 plan, originally proposed by Carmichael, Elder, and others to prepare undergraduate college teachers, has now received the endorsement of the Carnegie Forum Task Force on Teaching as a Profession (1986) and the Holmes Group, both of whom favor preservice teacher training at the graduate level.

The M.A.T. was meant to provide a terminal master's degree for secondary school teachers—a professional degree in the tradition of the M.B.A. or M.S.W. It paralleled experiments with the M.Phil. when high school and college teachers were in critically short supply and experiential degrees were in vogue. Unhappily, like the M.Phil., it appears in retrospect to have limited the career prospects of its recipients. Candidates for the M.A.T. tended to continue for the doctorate or to move from teaching into administration. The CGS Task Force on Concerns of Master's Degree–Granting Institutions (CGS 1981, p. 139) identified several issues facing teacher education: (1) the lack of institutional commitment or external funding for assistantships, facilities, and libraries; (2) the inadequacy of national ratings as evaluative criteria; (3) the unflattering profile of part-time students with their high rate of attrition; (4) the heavy teaching load of faculty with few grants; (5) the excessive attention given to course work rather than to research; and (6) the inconsistent requirements for the degree.

Most states require advanced training, classroom experience, and/or graduate course work for permanent or professional certification. As a result, the graduate student without any preprofessional training has many deficiencies that must be removed, thus lengthening the time and raising the cost of earning the degree. Only two states, Massachusetts and New Jersey, grant permanent licenses to first-year teachers upon completion of approved preparation programs; 13 require the master's degree for professional or permanent certification (Goertz 1986, p. 22). As graduate credits are linked to salary increments in most school districts and the B.A. plus 30 credits means a significant increase on the salary schedule, the impetus to acquire a master's degree has fiscal as well as career implications (Feistritzer 1983).

Both the Holmes Group and the Carnegie Forum mandate a master's degree for permanent certification. State departments of education are considering proposals for career ladder differentials into master teacher and other forms of recognition to forestall the ''up and out'' pattern now followed by better teachers who obtain sixth-year certificates to qualify as administrators. In many states, the only prerequisite to advancement into an administrative post is two years of classroom teaching, sometimes but not always linked to permanent teacher certification. Fifteen states now have career ladder or merit pay statutes as incentives to enter the profession. General salary increases and new minimum salaries have been implemented in more than 50 percent of them, scholarships and fellowships are being offered to preservice and master's level students in areas where teachers are in short supply, and 12 states have mandated support and evaluation systems for new teachers (Early 1985, p. iii). More than half the states have alternative certification mechanisms that vary from the traditional four-year college or university/two-year professional preparation sequence, including reductions in requirements for courses and field experience and paid internships in lieu of student teaching.

Thirty-seven states are studying or have adopted mandated changes in standards, ranging from discontinuance of programs that do not meet state criteria (Alabama and Georgia) to a four-step certification process that was on the state ballot in November 1986 (South Dakota) to a mandated reform package for all 66 colleges in Texas (Early 1985). One state, Washington, has recommended that teacher education be a two- to three-year postbaccalaureate professional program. And New York has begun a statewide formal review of 100 elementary education and bilingual education master's programs with the objective of terminating those that do not meet regulations in terms of students, faculty, curriculum, resources, facilities, and administration. It is also proposing an academic major for all undergraduates in teacher education, a one-year internship at the graduate level, and establishment of advanced professional classifications (Nolan 1986). Only one-fifth (223) of all schools, colleges, and departments of education accept freshmen into their undergraduate teacher education programs, more likely at private than public universities and colleges (Feistritzer 1983). Thirty-two states have now mandated that aspiring teachers pass a standardized test, such as the National Teachers' Examination Core Battery, to qualify for the provisional certificate (Goertz 1986, p. 24).

Since 1982, the American Association of Colleges of Teacher Education (AACTE) has issued a *Report to the Profession* about the institutional characteristics of its 722 member institutions. The report provides annual statistics on four levels of degrees (B.A., M.A., C.A.S., and Ph.D.) conferred in 18 specializations and in 15 content areas of secondary education. These data show the following changes between 1982 and 1984 at the master's level: 66 percent of member colleges offer the master's degree, 21 percent offer the doctorate, and all of those offering the Ph.D. or Ed.D. also offer master's degrees. The number of degrees conferred is used as the primary measure of productivity. The master's degree accounts for about 36 percent of all degrees awarded in education, but 26 percent fewer were awarded in schools, colleges, and departments of education accredited by the National Council for Accreditation of Teacher Education between 1982 and 1984. Elementary and secondary education, special education, and guidance attract most master's level students, and physical education is the most popular concentration in secondary education (*AACTE Briefs* 1984, p. 10). Between 1988 and 1992, the demand for new teachers will be 1.2 million and the supply will be 513,000, or 42.5 percent of the estimated need (Gerald 1985, p. 79). The many specialties in which teachers are now certified have resulted from federal policies that mandate such programs as compensatory education, programs for the handicapped, and bilingual education, strengthening demand for certified teachers in remedial and developmental subjects, special education, bilingual/bicultural education, and English as a second language. One field that has emerged as a result of federal legislation is adult education and community services. A survey of more than 100 adult education master's programs found little agreement on program requirements, including criteria for admission, core courses, concentrations, and methods of evaluation (Cameron 1984) and provides a good example of the confusion brought about by program diversity in one field. Titles alone vary from "adult and continuing education" to "adult education administration," "adult education leadership," "human resources development," and "gerontology." Fifty percent are offered off campus, the number of required courses varies from three to 30 credits, and the number of tracks and specializations varies from one to six or more. The types of required courses increase the number of variables—that is, foundations, planning, administration, and research.

Schools of education began to add "human services" or "human resources" in the late seventies and early eighties, reflecting changes in what constitutes teacher training as well as a pragmatic need to go beyond traditional pedagogy to work in nonschool settings. Graduate programs that meet the needs of business and industry for in-house corporate training have recently been added to the curriculum. And interest in critical thinking, problem solving, language and cognition, and education of the gifted and talented has grown.

Of the 1,287 schools, colleges, and departments of education in the United States (Feistritzer 1984), 682 offer the master's degree. They include 123 specialty areas in which fewer than 20 make awards (Golladay 1983, p. 11). Often the master's degree in education provides needed income to sustain costly doctoral programs, both in public universities where appropriations are linked to departmental full-time equivalent enrollments and in private universities and colleges that rely on tuition and fees to support their operating budgets. Although the bachelor's in education has declined relative to the master's degree, education ranks second to business in terms of total degrees awarded at all levels (17 percent compared to 21 percent of the total 1.26 million degrees awarded in 1980–81) (Golladay 1983, p. 2). The master's degree in education, however, leads business, 29.3 percent to 22.5 percent (OERI 1985). By 1982–83, almost half of all education degrees were graduate level, an increase from 35 percent in 1971 and much larger than for all other degrees (25 percent). Bachelor's degrees have been declining since 1973, and master's degrees, which had increased yearly until 1976, have now also begun to decline (Golladay 1983, p. 6). Doctorates have fluctuated since 1977. The proportion of graduate degrees in education earned by women has also increased, from 56 to 71 percent for the master's and from 21 to 47 percent for the doctorate. The diversity of the education degree with its 63 specialties is significant. Fourteen of them are in special education, which experienced a 123 percent increase in master's degrees since 1971 and in 1982–83 accounted for 13 percent of all master's degrees in education (OERI

1985). Other large specialties are student personnel, administration, and reading. The number of institutions awarding those degrees has also increased in the past decade, from 577 in 1971 to 683 in 1981. In the newest growth field, educational technology, 163 institutions offer 42 different majors, the most popular being computer-assisted instruction (Johnson 1985, p. 28).

Graduates of the University of Michigan's education programs were surveyed to determine patterns of degree study and subsequent career development of master's degree recipients (Stark and Austin 1982). Two groups were selected for study: 1969–70 graduates (when jobs were plentiful) and graduates from 1976 to 1981 (when jobs were scarce). Both claimed that their main reason for pursuing the degree was to improve professional skills or to obtain personal satisfaction. Applying credits already earned toward a degree, maintaining a job, or earning a certificate were least important. About one-third viewed transfer into a new profession as an important reason to obtain a degree, and one-half hoped a degree would eventually accelerate their advancement (p. 17). A survey of 1968 and 1969 graduates of nine Ford-sponsored M.A.T. programs that no longer exist and recent graduates of four current programs found that one-third of the first group are still teaching, while another 50 percent hold other jobs related to education (Coley and Thorpe 1986). Current M.A.T. students indicate they will enter and remain in teaching in the same proportions (p. 33). Efforts by the Carnegie Forum and the Holmes Group to convert the master's degree in teacher education into a first professional degree would raise it to a more advanced level and extend the time required for its completion.

A symposium on graduate teacher education in the eighties sought to address such issues as alternative educational agencies' offering inservice teacher training, the state's role in regulating and certifying teacher training programs, and the lack of differentiation between the M.A. and M.Ed. and Ph.D. and Ed.D. (Pipes 1979). Several panelists questioned the future of the master's degree, and one of them suggested that the incongruence between structures and purposes threatened to turn education degrees into nothing more than "artifacts" (Erdman 1979, pp. 61–62). The "increasing number and diversity of role specialties have had profound impact on proliferation of curricular content," so that instead of general principles of knowledge permeating the curriculum, extensive differentiation and duplication exist (p. 63).

Recent reports critical of elementary and secondary education have placed some of the blame for the schools' problems on the quality of teacher training programs, putting schools, colleges, and departments of education in a defensive position regarding the content of the degree, the mastery of that content, and the social and political implications of changes in the curriculum. Issues raised by the Carnegie Forum and other groups have focused on the lack of coherence in courses taken by professional degree candidates, the impact of the marketplace on the currency of the degree, the quality of students seeking careers in education, and the inconsistencies of certification requirements. The question is who should set the agenda for change—federal and state policy makers, local school systems, or the universities and their faculty. The outcome is likely to be a consensus among these constituencies as more public attention is focused on the reform of teacher education in the 1990s.

Engineering

The first engineering degree was an M.A. granted at Rensselaer Polytechnic Institute in 1824. Engineering programs became part of the college curriculum, however, following establishment of the land-grant universities under the Morrill Act of 1862. The American Society for Engineering Education (ASEE), established in 1893, formed the Committee on Engineering Degrees in 1910 and recommended that the first professional degree should lead to a Master of Science with designated specialty. The recommendation was never adopted. When the Engineers Council for Professional Development, now the Accreditation Board for Engineering and Technology (ABET), was organized in 1932 to oversee accreditation, it recommended that the degree indicate the level and specialty, for example, M.M.E., Master of Mechanical Engineering. For scientifically oriented curricula, the designation of M.S. was deemed sufficient (Ridley and Marchello 1985, p. 651). This recommendation, like its predecessor, was made in vain, and by 1963 degree designations in engineering outnumbered those in any other profession. ASEE made a third abortive attempt to restrict the number of master's degrees in 1964. Its Committee to Review Engineering Degrees suggested that only two be conferred at the master's level —the M.S. and the M.E., with designations in parentheses.

Now, however, 45 master's degree designations are possible in engineering and engineering technology, accounting for 7 percent of all master's degree titles (OERI 1985). In 1984, 135 out of 218 institutions offered the M.S., and 32 offered the M.E. and 15 other designations, including the M.S. in Teaching and the Master of Urban Systems Engineering. The popularity of engineering technology and engineering management programs, now numbering 80 (many of them for part-time students) has started a new round of degree proliferation. Some contend that no profession offers as many degree alternatives as engineering and that the lack of standardization and the continuing disagreement over titles and nomenclature are symptomatic of engineering's "failure to achieve full professional recognition, . . . the greatest deterrent to further development of the engineering profession" (Ridley and Marchello 1985, pp. 650, 653).

The issue is really quality control. The controversy over the differentiation in degree designations is linked to a perceived decline in standards and to persistent doubts that the engineering curriculum is sufficiently rigorous to meet objectives for a degree. ABET-accredited master's programs, however, presuppose a strong background in mathematics and science and are designed as advanced fifth-year programs for engineers or as one and one-half to two-year programs for nonengineering undergraduates. Two-thirds of the course work must be in advanced mathematics, basic sciences, engineering sciences, and engineering design; one-third must be in conceptual and integrative courses; and a thesis, research, or other special project is incorporated as the summative experience (ABET 1984, p. 7). Efforts have also been made, in the wake of the general concern over standards and the attainment of program objectives, to develop a continuum between undergraduate and graduate education, to extend the length of time for formal study, and to introduce more field experience.

The number of candidates for master's and professional engineering degrees declined in the 1970s but rose again in the 1980s, and enrollments have now stabilized at nearly 38,000 full-time and 32,000 part-time students (Ellis 1985, p. 104). About 12 percent of baccalaureates continue to the master's degree; about 18 percent of master's recipients continue to the doctorate. Electrical engineering is the most popular field, followed by mechanical, civil, and chemical engineering. Engineering degrees are the largest share of science/engineering master's degrees. Those earned by women increased from 10 percent in 1960 to 26 percent in 1980 (NSF 1985, p. 16). Master of Engineering programs that emphasize practice rather than research have had some success (Dieter 1984, p. 69). The Wang Institute of Graduate Studies and the National Technological University have taken the initiative in designing innovative master's programs in engineering (Eurich 1985). Speakers at a symposium on engineering in the 1980s asserted that traditional programs fail to meet the technological needs of society and must be redesigned to address problems of energy, transportation, communication, manufacturing, pollution, and engineering education (Engineering Foundation and ABET 1982). Recent advances in biotechnology and genetic engineering are not being adequately addressed because most schools of engineering have access to limited resources (Willenbrock 1985, p. 90). Further, engineering is the most popular field of study for foreign graduate students, mainly from third world countries in the Middle East and Asia, and foreign nationals now account for one-third of all master's students and one-half of all doctoral students in engineering (Ellis 1985, p. 108). This lack of American graduate students "degrad[es] the quality of undergraduate engineering" and contributes to the shortage of qualified engineering faculty with Ph.D.s (Willenbrock 1985, p. 90). The shortage is so acute that industry is prepared to attract qualified students into part-time engineering programs or traineeships, to finance basic and applied research, and to underwrite the costs of technology and laboratory equipment (Engineering Foundation and ABET 1982, pp. 23, 36). The employment of scientists and engineers in industry continues to grow by 7 percent each year, having more than doubled between 1973 and 1983 (NSF 1985).

. . . Foreign nationals now account for one-third of all master's students and one-half of all doctoral students in engineering.

Fine and Performing Arts

The Master of Fine Arts (M.F.A.) is a terminal degree awarded in the performing and visual arts, creative writing, and architecture. It is the preferred degree for the practicing artist, writer, musician, actor, or dancer and has greater status in the academic community than the M.A., considered a midpoint to the doctorate in arts and letters disciplines. Therefore, the artist as teacher has a greater opportunity for employment, promotion, and tenure in studio programs and courses. For this reason, too, schools of the arts have been established within universities to give greater standing to the creative fields and to permit more flexibility in designing and developing curricula.

A report on the status of M.F.A. degrees (Midwest College Art Conference 1965) and National Association of Schools of Art and Design (NASAD) guidelines indicate that the core of the M.F.A. program is the artistic discipline and that students are admitted based on the demonstrated quality and originality of their artistic output as well as their undergraduate grades. In some independent art schools, peer review is part of the admissions process. While the number of undergraduate credits in the field may vary as a criterion for admission, it is generally assumed that proficiency is a cumulative process, beginning before graduate school. Thus, students are rarely admitted de novo, implying that the graduate program will be structured at an advanced level, that a strong mentor-student relationship will exist, and that productivity will be expected. M.F.A. in visual arts programs require at least two years of full-time graduate study with a recommended 60 semester credit hours, at least 65 percent of which must be in studio practice (NASAD 1985, p. 74). The requirement for a thesis in M.F.A. programs is generally met by exhibition, performance, or comparable demonstration of achievement. Seventeen M.F.A. and eight M.A. programs are available in theater, 29 M.F.A. and eight M.A. programs in art/design, 23 M.M./M.F.A. programs and one M.A. in music, and seven M.F.A. and four M.A. programs in dance (HEADS 1985).

The number of specialties is extensive (HEADS 1985). The M.F.A. in theater includes 17 fields, ranging from act-

ing and costume design to theater management. In addition
to professional and academic studies, which occupy 75 percent of the curriculum, the National Association of Schools
of Theatre strongly recommends internships under professional conditions (1983, p. 55). The corresponding M.A.
degree with 65 percent theater content may include theater
education, history, playwriting, dramaturgy, and design.
Nearly 370 degrees were awarded in these fields in 1983–84
(HEADS 1985, chart 1–3). The M.F.A. in art/design
encompasses 29 specialties, ranging from advertising
design to visual communications and including glasswork-
ing, film, furniture design, and crafts. The corresponding
M.A. includes art education, administration, history, and
therapy. A total of 1,454 degrees in visual arts was
awarded in 1983–84 (HEADS 1985, chart 1–3).

The M.F.A. in music and the Master of Music (M.M.)
embrace 23 specializations in performance, composition,
and theory. A total of 3,389 degrees was offered in music,
the largest number of M.F.A. degrees awarded in 1983–84.
The M.F.A. in dance is the smallest field, with only 76
graduates in 1983–84, mainly in teaching specialties. This
program encompasses two years of full-time professional
practice in performance and choreography, culminating in
a final project demonstrating professional competence in
dance (NASD 1986, p. 53). The first M.F.A. program in
creative writing—the Iowa Writers Workshop—was established in 1936 at Iowa State University, whose Department
of English in the 1920s had already granted the first
advanced degrees in critical and creative writing (Howard
1986, p. 34). More than 150 graduate writing programs are
now available in the United States, at least 100 "born in
the last decade" (p. 34).

In developing standards of accreditation, it has been recommended that the M.F.A. degree be reserved for those
programs that emphasize practice of the art form toward a
professional career as artist, musician, dancer, actor, or
writer and that the M.A. degree be granted for programs
whose major emphasis is history, educational theory, and
research. This recommendation implies that the teaching
faculty of the M.F.A. program will be predominantly
active professionals whose work commands attention in
exhibition, performance, production, or print or in applied

fields whose work is used commercially. The Yale School of Art is an example of the benefits to be derived from a distinguished faculty of professional artists (Sandler 1982). In fact, a direct correlation has been found between the quality and reputation of M.F.A. programs and their ability to attract the most promising students (Hathaway 1975).

Health Sciences

Nursing
The University of Minnesota established the first school of nursing and Teachers College the first department of nursing and health in 1909 (AACN 1985). As a largely female occupation based on a medical model and dominated initially by physicians, it has not had the status of other professional programs. Apprenticeship is part of its heritage, and training has occurred mainly through clinical programs in hospitals (NLN 1978, p. 30). A unified accreditation process under the aegis of several nursing organizations was initiated in 1947, the National League of Nursing in 1952, and the American Association of Colleges of Nursing in 1969. Evaluation of baccalaureate and master's programs began in the late 1950s, and as of 1984, 157 master's programs were available in departments of nursing (NLN 1984, p. 51).

Nursing is a profession dominated by registered nurses, 80 percent of whom lack advanced degrees (Hart 1981, p. 33). Only 5 percent of nurses have master's degrees, only 1 percent doctorates (AACN 1985, p. 4). It was not until 1981 that the three national organizations—NLN, AACN, and the American Nursing Association (ANA)—publicly stated the need to make advanced training a first priority (Murphy 1981, p. 3). In the 1950s and 1960s, graduate nursing programs emphasizing preparation of nurse teachers often neglected theory and practice (Kelley 1981, p. 4).

The first regional effort by four public and two private universities to plan joint graduate programs in nursing occurred in the mid-1950s under the aegis of the Southern Regional Education Board (NLN 1980, p. 1). Generous capitation funding through the Nurse Training Act of 1964 accelerated the growth of basic nursing programs. Only in the 1980s, however, has nursing begun to experience a major thrust in the training of graduate nursing leaders. The NLN's Council of Baccalaureate and Higher Degree Programs defines the Master of Science in Nursing (M.S.N.) as a specialization program based on an upper-division major in nursing as the first professional degree. The purpose is to prepare professional nursing leaders as clinical specialists (practitioners), teachers, supervisors, and administrators. NLN-accredited programs combine study in a clinical area (family, child, surgical, psychiatric, or community health nursing) with study of a functional role, such as clinician, teacher, supervisor, or administrator. The graduate M.S.N. seeks to build professional skills on a theoretical foundation, differentiating this degree from earlier hospital-based programs. NLN's new criteria on "Characteristics of Graduate Education in Nursing Leading to the Master's Degree" stress graduate study as part of a continuum with the upper-division major in nursing, making it difficult for the R.N. without a baccalaureate in nursing to enroll. The master's degree is construed as an advanced, specialized training program in which the functional role and the clinical specialty are an organic whole, delineated clearly in curriculum design and content (NLN 1980). This two-year degree may vary from 36 to 60 credits and may also require a practicum, comprehensive examination, and in some cases a thesis.

Nursing, like other degrees, has wrestled with the issue of nomenclature. Master's degree titles include M.S., M.A., M.N., and M.S.N., and several interesting issues have been raised in this context: (1) the lack of differentiation between designations and requirements for a degree; (2) the relationship between professional nursing programs and the schools that house them; and (3) restrictive admissions requirements that specify an upper-division major in nursing, deterring enrollment of community college graduates and R.N.s with bachelor's degrees in other fields (Murphy 1981, p. 5). Less than one-fourth of all nurses now have four-year degrees, accentuating the gatekeeping function of accreditation criteria. As a result, the profession is now addressing several major issues: (1) what constitutes the first professional degree in nursing; (2) whether nonnurses should be allowed to earn the M.S.N. and gain eligibility for the same license; (3) whether the M.S.N. should represent a higher level of knowledge and clinical expertise than the B.S.N.; and (4) how to differentiate the R.N. with a baccalaureate in another field, a B.S.N., and a nonnursing major in professional M.S.N. programs. The University of Tennessee offers three separate tracks or concentrations, lengthening the time to degree for the non-nursing group to achieve an M.S.N. (Hart 1981, p. 34).

An analysis of job market trends for nurses questions the role of the master's degree to prepare clinical specialists (Balint, Menninger, and Hurt 1983). Almost half the available jobs advertised in 26 professional nursing journals for a three-year period were for educational positions, 50.7 percent of them requiring a doctorate; however, most nurses were in clinical programs, which accounted for only 7 percent of advertised jobs (p. 111).

AACN studies address the need for innovation and change in nursing education arising out of the new demography of the profession, the growth of part-time, nontraditional student populations, and the diversification of the health care industry. Community-based outreach programs, evening and weekend programs, and multidisciplinary and bilateral arrangements with industry, hospitals, and mental health agencies are some of the models discussed. The Nursing Curriculum Project of the Southern Regional Education Board identifies such future directions as outreach models, interdisciplinary health education, consortia, health marketing, health resources management, and the dual functions of practice and teaching in a generic nursing curriculum (Kelley 1981, p. 5). Massachusetts General Hospital has designed the MGH Institute of Health Professions to integrate programs within a noncollegiate clinical setting (Porter 1982, p. 42). It grants master's degrees in nursing, dietetics, physical therapy, and speech-language pathology, stressing multidisciplinary approaches and cooperation among disciplines (Eurich 1985, p. 119).

Between 1964 and 1984, the number of graduate nursing programs grew from 53 to 157 out of 380 AACN member schools. Enrollments reached 19,086 students, 68.3 percent of whom were part time, a trend that has been continuing since 1967, except in the West. The total number of degrees dropped by 2.1 percent, to 5,039, as a result of the increase in part-time enrollments. Seventy percent of the graduates were in advanced clinical practice (one-third in medical-surgical nursing), 16.4 percent in teaching, and

12.2 percent in administration/management, the three functional areas for which data are provided (NLN 1984). The results showed 6.6 times as many baccalaureate as master's degree recipients.

The existing confusion in nursing education about appropriate conceptual frameworks for undergraduate and graduate curricula is not surprising when one reflects on the historical development of graduate nursing education. Originally, it emphasized functional preparation for nurse-teachers, and programs consequently were often housed in schools, colleges, or departments of education. Four courses were considered essential in the early graduate programs: philosophy of education, curriculum development, teaching strategies, and tests and measurements (Kelley 1981, p. 4). "Application of the science of teaching to the practice of nursing [,however,] was often lacking" (p. 4). In the sixties, with pressure from NLN, programs were revised to meet the needs of nurse-practitioners. The concept of the sixth-year certificate or a two-year program for teachers was also proposed. The issue today is how to meet the needs of the part-time adult student who may not have studied nursing as an undergraduate, has many more professional specializations from which to select, and whose training should reflect the diversification of the health care industry and the dual functions of practice and teaching (Hart 1981; Kelley 1981).

Health services administration
The first master's degree in hospital administration was initiated at the University of Chicago in 1934. By 1978, more than 70 graduate programs (43 fully accredited) were available in hospital or health administration, public health administration, and health planning, paralleling the growth of publicly and privately financed medical care in the 1960s (Moyerman 1978, p. 1). A CGS workshop on master's degrees pointed out that allied health comprises 35 different professions with 38 sets of accreditation standards administered by seven agencies, one of which has 16 committees (CGS 1983, p. 31). The Association of University Programs in Health Administration has attempted to remedy this situation by serving as an umbrella association for public health administration.

Public health administration is a two-year interdisciplinary degree, incorporating components from medicine, engineering, epidemiology, organizational behavior, accounting, financial management, and statistics. Three months to one year of field work as an administrative resident in a health facility may be integrated into requirements for the degree. The programs have various titles and about 12 designations (in order of frequency): Master of Health/Health Services Administration; M.B.A. in Health Administration; Master of Public Administration; Master of Public Health; Master of Science in Hospital, Hospital and Health Services, or Health Care Administration; Master of Management in Hospital and Health Services Administration (Filerman 1981, pp. 3–4). The absence of a commonly labeled degree presents problems to students trying to select the right program and to potential employers trying to understand what the degrees mean. To complicate the matter further, health programs may be housed in schools of business, public health, public administration, medicine and allied health, or as separate university departments, and the program's emphasis correlates closely with its university affiliation. The American Physical Therapy Association has mandated that by 1990 all entry-level programs be postbaccalaureate. As the only accrediting agency in this field, with eligibility for licensure and practice depending on graduation from an accredited program, allied health administrators will be faced with the prospect of adding new master's programs in physical therapy. An analogous situation has occurred in rehabilitation counseling. According to 1984 certification guidelines, programs with fewer than 48 credits are not fully accredited by the Commission on Rehabilitation Education (CORE). CORE-approved programs include a 600-hour supervised internship that qualifies master's degree recipients to sit for Commission on Rehabilitation Counseling Certification without experience in the field (CRCC 1984, p. 4). A study of health administration curricula to determine whether they meet professional needs and are responsive to societal and institutional change concludes that they often develop "by accretion and eclectic borrowing of courses from other established disciplines" (Moyerman 1978, p. 2). Degree requirements are based on state and national standards and institutional resources.

A case study of a new two-year master's degree in health policy and management established by Harvard's School of Public Health provides a different perspective on the development of degrees in this field (Harvard University School of Public Health 1978). With support from the National Institutes of Health (NIH), the school convened 12 panels on various public health concerns, asking them to define personnel and organizational needs in a changing health care delivery system. The Health Services and Environmental Health panels identified training health policy analysis managers as the primary need and urged the school to focus the degree in this area. After five years of planning, implementation, and evaluation, such a degree was instituted in collaboration with the Business School and the Kennedy School of Government. Initiated in 1973, it was combined with the M.S. in health services administration two years later. It is open to doctors and postbaccalaureates seeking entry to health-related careers and provides a model of what can be achieved with sufficient resources, meticulous planning, and clear and purposeful objectives. Quality has not been sacrificed to ad hoc invention.

It . . . provides a model of what can be achieved with sufficient resources, meticulous planning, and clear and purposeful objectives.

International Education

International education has three main foci—schools of international affairs, area centers funded through Title VI of the Higher Education Act of 1965, and foreign language departments with links to both schools and centers. International studies programs generally lead to the M.A., combining fluency in a language with multidisciplinary training in history, institutions, and culture, and preparing students for employment in government and the private sector (Berryman et al. 1979, p. 33). More recently, their curricula have emphasized quantitative analysis, economics, and business, particularly in schools of international affairs. In recognition of the growing importance of international business and international law, some university language departments and area centers are now seeking cross-fertilization with business and law schools, and joint programs with law are common.

Schools of international studies like the Fletcher School of Law and Diplomacy at Tufts, which offers the Master of Arts in Law and Diplomacy (M.A.L.D.), and the Woodrow Wilson School of Public and International Affairs at

Princeton operate largely as autonomous units, produce mostly M.A.s, and concentrate on internationl policy (Berryman et al. 1979, p. 37). Particular attention is given to research skills that can be applied to emerging international problems in the environment, energy, and health. Title VI centers were designed originally to train specialists as technical advisors in predominantly third world countries, and the average number of M.A.s awarded through these centers is from two to 82 per center (Schneider 1985). In 1981–83, most degrees were awarded in Latin American, East Asian, or international studies, often combined with an M.B.A., J.D., or M.P.H. Area centers encourage integrated or combined degrees that are consistent with Title VI legislation.

Journalism
The debate over journalism as a professional degree erupted in the 1930s (Dressel 1960, p. 25). Schools of journalism were denounced, both for their narrow focus and for their vocationalism (Flexner 1930; Hutchins 1936). In 1930, the American Society of Newspaper Editors recommended that they become graduate level, offering the master's as the first professional degree. Columbia established the first graduate school of journalism in 1935, replacing its earlier conventional master's degree (30 credits plus an examination and thesis) with an intensive five-year program (Baker 1954, p. iii). The only other exclusively graduate school of journalism is at UCLA. Northwestern has a 3-2 program leading to an M.S. in journalism. The Accrediting Council on Education in Journalism and Mass Communications, which began formal accreditation of journalism programs in 1945, represents 25 member organizations in publishing, mass communications, and electronic journalism.

Over 300 schools and departments now offer graduate and undergraduate programs in journalism and mass communications, including concentrations in diverse occupational specialties of news-editorial (newspapers), advertising, broadcasting, public relations, magazine, community, technical, science, agriculture, and home economics journalism, journalism research, legal journalism (sometimes part of an M.S./J.D.), and Afro-American journalism. Graduate enrollments are only 10 percent of the total, although four times as many advanced degrees were awarded in 1982 as in 1965 (Peterson 1985, p. 5). Forty-five schools awarded 50 or more advanced degrees in 1983–84. The trend continues from editorial journalism to nontraditional sequences, particularly electronic media (p. 3). The M.A. is still the preferred degree designation. A by-product of the popularity of this field is the introduction by graduate departments of English of modified programs in journalism and mass communications as a means of diversifying their traditional curriculum for students not interested in pursuing a doctorate and giving a more vocational cast to the humanities.

Two types of graduate degree programs are offered: an intensive one-year degree for those with no undergraduate background in journalism and a specialized program for baccalaureates in journalism or mass communications. Scholarly and professional publications have paid little attention to graduate study apart from case studies of individual programs, discussions of admissions criteria, and enrollment surveys. An analysis of 77 master's programs found considerable diversity in definition, quality, structure, and students' backgrounds as well as a general absence of substantive research on the relationship of journalism as a field of study to the profession (Ryan 1980). Diversity among students is a function of undergraduate preparation and the work experience of those who enroll— that is, the baccalaureate seeking an entry-level job in the media, the experienced journalist seeking to improve his or her skills or to move into another field in the media, the baccalaureate in mass communications seeking a fifth year of study, or the doctoral candidate interested in theory and research (pp. 32–33). This diversity limits the usefulness of Graduate Record Examination (GRE) scores and undergraduate grades as criteria for admission, a problem shared by other professional schools with mixed cohorts of post-baccalaureate and mid-career students. Students' diversity has led to curricular diversity, with a profusion of specialties and a consequent loss of definition and quality.

Law
Harvard granted the Master of Laws to those who completed the LL.B. with distinction. Columbia awarded the first earned LL.M. in 1864. Only one first professional degree exists in law—the Juris Doctor (previously the

LL.B.). It was not until 1896 that an undergraduate degree was required for admission to law schools, elevating it to its current status of first professional degree. The American Bar Association takes the position that no graduate degree in law—LL.M., M.C.L., or S.J.D.—is or should be a substitute for the first professional degree in law and that no graduate degree should qualify as meeting the legal education requirements for admission to the bar (ABA 1984). The three-year course of study leading to the first degree is a generalist program to educate the student in the disciplines required in legal practice.

Increased specialization has led law schools to offer post-J.D. programs that are professional rather than academic in content and objectives. An ABA survey indicates that 59 law schools offer 56 different specializations (Ruud 1985), ranging from admiralty, banking, and criminal law to mental health, taxation, and trade regulation. Twenty schools offer individually structured programs tailored to students' interests. The most common designation is the LL.M. Others are Master of Comparative Law (M.C.L.), Master of Arts or Science in Legal Institutions (M.L.I.), Master of Comparative Jurisprudence (M.C.J.), and Master of Asian Law (M.A.L.S.). All programs require 20 to 24 credits of concentrated courses, culminating in a seminar. Law schools in cooperation with other schools offer joint degrees in 28 areas (and 102 subfields), ranging from the Master of Law in Labor and Industrial Relations (M.A.L.I.R.) to world politics.

Library Science
Melvil Dewey established the first library school in 1887, the School of Library Economy at Columbia. In 1902, it became a graduate-level program and along with others laid the foundation for the American system of library schools (Wilson 1970, p. 45). The American Association of Library Schools (AALS) was formed in 1919; in 1925, it appointed the Board of Education for Librarianship (BEL) to administer standards for six types of schools, among them graduate library schools offering one-year certificates and advanced graduate library schools conferring master's and doctoral degrees. Some consideration had already been given to the possibility of a two-year master's in library science. In 1924, the BEL had requested guidance

on this subject from the AAU Committee on Academic and Professional Higher Degrees, which recommended a two-year M.A. or M.S., the former for vocational courses leading to a certificate and the latter for graduate scholarly work. It rejected the proposal of a fifth-year bachelor's degree. The agreement that was eventually reached endorsed the use of the B.S., B.A., M.S., and M.A. with or without the qualifying phrase "in library science" until graduate programs could be implemented (Darling 1980, p. 3).

The first M.L.S. was offered at the University of Colorado in 1947; Peabody College (Vanderbilt) offered the first fifth-year master's degree (Gleaves 1982, p. 271). Before that time, the fifth year of study had led to a second bachelor's degree, the B.L.S. New curricular standards adopted by the American Library Association (ALA) in 1951 made the M.L.S. the first professional degree upon completion of the approved five-year program (Yungmyer 1984, p. 110), and requirements were restated to place preprofessional, professional, and graduate professional studies in a logical order (Wilson 1970, p. 58). The ALA encouraged concentration of professional library training in the fifth year, and by 1955, all ALA-accredited schools followed this model. By 1980, 62 accredited M.L.S. programs were offered, a 60 percent increase since 1967, and only 17 were private (Gleaves 1982, p. 266). The M.L.S. was elevated to the level of first professional degree for several reasons: (1) to transmit an advanced body of knowledge and technical skill in specialized areas; (2) to improve professional practice through a critical approach to librarianship; and (3) to raise the status and standards of librarianship as a profession (Berelson 1970, p. 207).

Graduate enrollments in library science declined in the late seventies, but they now appear to have stabilized at about 4,000. Some believed that existing M.L.S. programs would introduce new concentrations, particularly in information science and information management, to expand enrollments and respond to a changing labor market but that entirely new programs were not likely to be sanctioned, to avoid the problem of more graduates than jobs (Gleaves 1982, p. 265). Meanwhile, the trend to joint degrees continued. A survey of research librarians identified 20 disciplines that were combined with M.L.S. programs, the most popular being history, law, and business (Marchant and Wilson 1983, p. 31). Other joint degrees were combined with education, archives, area studies, music, art, and English. The library directors felt that, while the second degree is a useful supplement to the M.L.S., two degrees earned independently have greater validity. Indiana University's School of Library and Information Science has combined the M.L.S. with advanced degrees in musicology, history, public affairs, science, journalism, and art history (Dewey 1985, pp. 431–32). All of these dual degrees consist of 30 credits in library/information science, 20 to 33 credits in the parallel master's, and a practicum in the appropriate library, for example, archives, government documents, or fine arts (p. 431).

The academic and economic implications of extending the M.L.S. from a one-year, 36-credit degree to a two-year, 60-credit program were debated vigorously in 1980 as a result of the *Conant Report* (1980). The ALA Executive Board and the Wilson Foundation had commissioned Conant in 1972 to assess professional library education. The subsequent analysis strongly supported the development of a two-year degree on the assumption that a professional program must serve three functions: (1) to determine who enters the profession and what qualifications and standards are met to qualify for professional practice; (2) to provide formal instruction for those seeking to qualify for professional practice; and (3) to supply the profession with qualified people, continuing their education, defining the objectives of the profession, and anticipating future needs (Conant 1980, p. 13).

Measured against these criteria, the one-year M.L.S. is inadequate (Conant 1980), offering only "the basics of librarianship," equating graduate training with elementary courses, limiting opportunities for specialization, precluding an internship or work-study program, limiting faculty-student interaction, and leading to a "quick" degree reflecting adversely on the profession (p. 24). In fact, of the 68 ALA-accredited graduate library schools, 66 adhere to the one- to one and one-half–year model with no introductory undergraduate work—precisely the model Conant abhorred. Emphasis is on the basic components—reference, bibliography, technical courses, and administration—and concentrations are offered in academic, school, or public librarianship, information science, research methods, and client group services. To give students the opportunity to specialize, basic requirements are minimal.

For Conant, research universities and first-rank professional schools emphasize theory and principles, comprehensive universities vocational content and practical training (p. 53). The latter attract students with routine career goals—operative, paraprofessional, entry level. The more elite schools emphasize skills in leadership. Most professions rely on their educational institutions to train new professionals, carry out research, anticipate new areas of service, and enhance professional practice (p. 56). Recognizing that library accreditation was to some extent a political process certifying institutional achievement and legitimizing its schools and programs, Conant proposed a two-year professional training program for those assuming leadership positions and a one-year program for school and public librarians—a dual-track system distinguishing at the institutional level between paraprofessional and management positions (p. 194). UCLA was the first to adopt a two-year program, partly in response to a felt need among its faculty for fewer, better-trained library professionals (Hayes 1980, p. 46) and partly to complement its one-year Master of Science in Information Science (M.S.I.S.) degree. By adopting a two-year program, it was able to add more specialization in information science (as Conant himself had urged), a research thesis, and an internship to test it in practice (an organic relationship between theory and practice). The two-year degree also gave greater flexibility in offering cognate courses than the tightly structured one-year degree.

Some library schools now offer a sixth-year Certificate of Advanced Study (C.A.S.) consisting of eight to ten courses in a specialization. All of these developments are harbingers of change in the concept and role of the professional librarian and constitute a severe challenge to traditional schools and departments.

Public Administration
Of the 211 schools listed in the most recent directory of the National Association of Schools of Public Affairs and Administration (NASPAA), 199 offer the master's degree. Thirty-eight of these programs are located within political

science departments, 26 are separate professional schools, 64 are separate departments of public administration, and 26 are combined with a school or department of business. Total enrollments were 21,158 in 1983, 65 percent of them part time and 68 percent in-service. The most popular degree is the Master of Public Administration (M.P.A.), representing 77 percent of all degrees awarded, but the Master of Municipal Public Administration (M.M.P.A.), Master of Urban Affairs (M.U.A.), and Master of Public Policy (M.P.P.) are also popular. Almost 70 percent of graduates are in government agencies; only 4 percent continue their education to the Doctor of Public Administration (D.P.A.) or the Ph.D. A large number of diverse specializations are subsumed under public administration and public affairs, including arts policy and planning, human resource management, labor relations, public policy analysis, justice administration, and health services management. OERI's new taxonomy includes social work degrees in this category (see footnote, p. 3).

In 1986, NASPAA issued amended "Standards for Professional Master's Degree Programs in Public Affairs and Administration," forming the framework for the design of graduate programs and delineating curricula and general competencies to produce professionals capable of assuming leadership and management roles in public policy and administration (p. 1). The curriculum is comprised of a common core for all public affairs and administration programs—for example, quantitative analysis and organizational theory, additional components already identified in the common core, and work in an established area of concentration or specialization chosen by the student. Thus, the student combines generic foundation courses with specialization in a subfield of the discipline. Common components of the curriculum are designed to enable the student to gain understanding of the environment in which public policy operates and the expertise to deal with political, legal, economic, and social institutions and processes, concepts of organization and management (including human resource administration), concepts and techniques of financial administration, and techniques of analysis (including quantitative, econometric, and statistical methods). Specific courses may be prescribed, or students may select from clusters of courses. The guidelines mandate that common components be covered by required prerequisites and/ or graduate work, however. Additional components of the curriculum in specialization and concentration courses may not be substituted for the common core. In addition to these elements, students are expected to develop competencies in data collection, analysis, and communication, considered a major function of the public administrator.

NASPAA encourages specializations that meet the needs of public administrators who may be engineers, health care administrators, or employees of a nonprofit agency. A handbook prepared jointly by the American Public Works Association (APWA) and NASPAA provides guidelines for developing a master's degree specialization in public works administration within the M.P.A. It suggests five operational ways to serve this sector: (1) by increasing public works technology and practice in the engineering curriculum; (2) by including public administration and social science subject matter and a major in public works planning and management in the engineering curriculum; (3) by encouraging graduate students in engineering and other fields (environmental science, public health, urban planning, architecture) to earn a dual or sequential master's degree or certificate in public administration, urban management, or public policy; (4) by recruiting more preservice and mid-career engineers and scientists for enrollment in public affairs/policy/administration/management programs; and (5) by initiating collaborative arrangements that involve a school of public administration and school of engineering (APWA/NASPAA 1983).

Innovative programs stressing self-directed learning have made few inroads into the M.P.A. (Zottoli 1984). A few programs whose major purpose is to train practitioners have endeavored to recruit students with relevant work experience, offering academic credit for substantial management experience. New York University offers a 60-credit M.P.A. program exclusively on Saturdays that can be completed within two and one-half years. A 32-credit M.S. in management program on Saturdays for professionals with degrees in law, medicine, engineering, education, and accounting emphasizes health services and management in the nonprofit sector.

Social Work

While the first university-affiliated programs in social work were established in 1904 in New York, Boston, and Chicago, it was not until 1932 that the American Association of Schools of Social Work (AASSW) set a minimum one-year curriculum as the first uniform standard of courses and fieldwork for the degree. By 1939, the two-year graduate degree had become the AASSW standard (Dinerman and Geismar 1984, p. 34). The basic curriculum emphasized casework and sometimes group work and community organization, not administration or research. The National Association of Social Work, established in 1955, adopted the M.S.W. as the preferred credential for a social service professional. Through federal action, the field was transformed, schools of social work expanded, more B.S.W. programs established, and new models of practice initiated in community action, policy analysis, and urban affairs (Gurin and Williams 1973, p. 209). In 1959, 52 accredited schools of social work existed; by 1985, 90 (with nine more candidates) and four levels of education in social work—A.A., B.S.W., M.S.W., and Ph.D. or D.S.W.— existed. Public policy had created entirely new specifications and with them a huge number of new jobs and training modules. The addition of undergraduate B.S.W. degrees in social work and A.A. and B.S. degrees in human services elevated the two-year M.S.W. to a second professional degree, encouraged a 4-1 model for B.S.W.s continuing to the master's degree, and introduced many subspecialties, leading to a proliferation of courses and degrees (Dinerman 1982).

The M.S.W. has declined since the late 1960s.

From the early 1950s to the early 1970s, the M.S.W. was the degree of entry into the profession, the degree recognized as a condition of membership in NASW, and the only degree accredited by CSWE. In addition, the M.S.W. degree was the standard promoted by the profession to the general public as the educational requirement for professional social work practice (Humphreys and Dinerman 1984, p. 196).

In the past decade, the largest growth has been at the undergraduate level, although it was not until 1974 that the Council on Social Work Education (CSWE) began accrediting such programs in recognition of the need to implement standards for preprofessional preparation and to strengthen the articulation between degree levels.

In 1984, 14,275 full-time and 7,294 part-time M.S.W. candidates were enrolled, compared to only 4,778 in 1959 (Rubin 1985, p. 35). Full-time enrollments peaked at almost 18,000 in 1978, after increasing annually for two decades. Part-time enrollments continue to grow, however, and now account for one-third of all master's students. Paralleling the decline in full-time M.S.W. enrollments, the number of degrees awarded in 1984 dropped to 8,053, 11 percent below 1983 but four times higher than in 1959. Social work is a predominantly female profession: 78.9 percent of all M.S.W. degrees are awarded to women (pp. 38–39).

The diversification of the work force has been linked to confusion about the meaning of the M.S.W. (Humphreys and Dinerman 1984, pp. 196–98). New criteria for entry through the rapid expansion of B.S.W.s, outside pressures from human service occupations, and the elimination of Title XX and various public programs have created competition between B.S.W.s and M.S.W.s and confusion about their respective skills and roles. Efforts to define the basic B.S.W. curriculum and to differentiate it from the M.S.W. have been underway since 1975. A survey of B.S.W. and M.S.W. programs found enormous diversity within and across degree levels to the extent that "the degree level is not a predictor of the extent of exposure to any content or the focus of content that a graduate will have had" (Dinerman 1982, p. 89). The B.S.W. and M.S.W. offer duplicate and overlapping courses and omit others, raising important questions about the function of the degree. Is its purpose to impart a common core of knowledge and skills for all social workers, and if not is it a single profession or many variations on one? What outcomes do we expect from the M.S.W. without a B.S.W. and from the B.S.W./M.S.W. as a continuum? Is the undergraduate experience a "discontinuous model," or is it a continuum where "specialized becomes advanced education based on a shared foundation" (p. 91)? Perhaps it would be preferable to reverse the B.S.W. generalist/M.S.W. specialist continuum, providing specific knowledge and skills in B.S.W. programs and a higher level of abstraction in theoretical, research-based M.S.W. programs (Hartman 1983, p. 27).

Accreditation standards for both the B.S.W. and M.S.W.

Is its purpose to impart a common core of knowledge and skills for all social workers, and if not is it a single profession or many variations on one?

---

as set forth by CSWE require five components—research, human behavior and social environment, social welfare policy and services, social work practice, and the field practicum (Ewalt 1983). Emphases vary considerably between degree levels, however. The M.S.W. is more analytical than descriptive, courses are more specialized than generic, and the number of credits to degree ranges from 55 to 90, compared to 125 for the B.S.W. with a liberal arts base (Dinerman 1982, pp. 86–88).

Detailed guidelines for developing and evaluating the two-year degree (Ewalt 1983, chap. 1) perceive the domain for review of the curriculum as a transactional system in which the components (objectives, outcomes, concentrations, sequences, and courses) are linked to educational and social contexts, including students' characteristics, employment, and societal needs (p. 5). One of the confusing elements is that no single principle had been adopted for organizing the curriculum. Concentrations may be organized by field of practice (health or criminal justice, for example), methodology (administration, planning), age cohort (child, family, elderly), ethnic population, or social problem (drugs), for advanced generalists, or as a combination (p. 23). This diversity gives students many choices, but it may also lead to a disunified curriculum and to a proliferation of courses, programs, and ultimately degrees. Despite all of these choices, most M.S.W. students (98.4 percent) select a methods concentration (Rubin 1985, pp. 41–44); over two-thirds combine it with a field of practice or concentration in a social problem. The most frequently selected methods concentration is direct practice (51 percent), and fewer than 2 percent of all students concentrate solely in a field of practice or social problem. Mental health is the most prominent field of practice, followed by health, family services, child welfare, and aging.

Financial aid is a major incentive to obtain the degree in a field that is not highly remunerative. Almost 50 percent of full-time students receive grants, 11 percent from field agencies (Rubin 1985, p. 47). The most common source of federal funds not tied to field instruction is formal loan programs (36.5 percent of all grants awarded to M.S.W. students), followed by school or university grants (26.2 percent) and college work study (8.3 percent). The decline in M.S.W. applicants has been ascribed to low salaries, uncertain employment, the high cost of education, declining financial aid, and a shift in society's values from social reform and community action to more utilitarian goals (Carbino and Morgenbesser 1982, p. 16), and the trend is expected to continue through this decade (Rubin 1985). As a profession allied with the public sector, social work depends on political decision making. The lack of employment opportunities caused by retrenchment of domestic programs has discouraged potential students from seeking M.S.W. degrees (Born 1982, p. 7). "Educational design in professional programs must be related to manpower and employment, and vice versa" (Dinerman 1982, p. 92).

Combined Degrees

Combined, dual, or joint degrees enable students to work toward degrees in more than one field simultaneously and in a highly structured, time-shortened mode of study. Thus, requirements for admission are apt to be more rigorous and selective, students more highly motivated and with more diverse interests and goals, and institutional resources more fully used. Peterson's Guides (Goldstein and Frary 1985) list 155 combined degrees, joining two master's, a master's and a first professional, or a master's and a Ph.D. Thirteen fields are most often involved—architecture, biomedical sciences, business administration, engineering, health administration, journalism, law, library science, medicine, public health, public policy and administration, social work, and urban and regional planning. The most popular combined degrees involve law, business, and medicine and range from the M.S./M.D. to the M.B.A./J.D. Esoteric combinations include the M.L.I.S./M.A. in information science and Near Eastern studies, the M.P.L./M.S.G. in urban and regional planning and gerontology, and the M.S.W./M.S. in social work and dance therapy.

Innovation and change can be viewed as a continuum ranging from the introduction of new courses of study to the restructuring of disciplines and entire academic units. The impetus for recent innovation derived from external forces that fostered the expansion of public and private higher education, supported experimental programs, encouraged access and opportunity, and created a receptive environment for change.

A useful analysis of interdisciplinary science asserts that the "introduction of new and different sets of conceptual models in organizing information provides one of the best avenues of innovation" (Roy 1979, p. 191). It theorizes that the major research universities of the 21st century will be organized to accommodate "both discipline-oriented and mission-oriented entities" as a result of several factors (p. 193): a recognition among faculty that social and technological problem solving cannot occur in "discipline-shaped blocks" labeled chemistry, geology, or economics (p. 165); the explosion of knowledge in the basic and applied sciences; and the need to provide students with the intellectual resources to avoid "superspecialization," to understand relationships among "federations of disciplines," and to prepare for occupational changes throughout their productive lives.

Change comes in two categories in the eighties: (1) administrative change, which has led to joint degree programs, consortia, self-directed study, and external degrees; and (2) curricular change that focuses on new disciplines, new scholarship, and new ideas (Solmon 1984, p. 23). The use of cost-benefit analyses can be a basis for strengthening existing graduate programs rather than replacing them with new ones (p. 29). The danger lies in not providing adequate institutional incentives to support continued innovation. As external sources of support have diminished in the 1980s, education has entered a time of retrenchment linked to managing enrollments, developing career programs, and adhering to external and institutional standards of excellence. But four "disincentives to change" go beyond cost-benefit analysis: (1) greater status for theoretical than applied programs, vertical specialization than breadth, and established than emergent programs; (2) the greater likelihood of confusing packaging with substance, delivery systems with content, and structures with goals;

(3) structural barriers between master's and doctoral programs, academic and applied disciplines, graduate and professional education; and (4) continued preoccupation with quality and standards, generating retrenchment and consolidation instead of innovation and change (Albrecht 1984, p. 11).

The most common type of innovative graduate program is the interdisciplinary degree that combines subject matter fields around a common theme and seeks to transform the curriculum by infusing new knowledge into existing disciplines. In 1982–83, 3,819 degrees were awarded in liberal studies and interdisciplinary studies, including system studies, ethnic studies, and peace studies (OERI 1985). Women's studies provides an excellent example of the rationale and design of interdisciplinary programs at the graduate level. A review of 53 graduate programs indicates that many models exist for M.A. degrees in women's studies (MLA 1986b, p. 655). They combine course work in literature, language, or art with work in sociology, anthropology, economics, political science, history, philosophy, psychology, biology, and related fields. Programs are organized to offer autonomous M.A. degrees in women's studies, liberal studies, American studies, and interdisciplinary studies or as concentrations within a major in literature, history, or social or behavioral science. Some schools offer individualized, self-directed study leading to the M.A. degree in a discipline with emphasis on women's studies.

Women's studies programs question traditional assumptions about the structure, content, theories, and teaching practices underlying academic disciplines, and its adherents seek nothing less than transformation of the curriculum through the infusion of new material, perspectives, and methods of research and teaching. They are critical of the core curriculum as perpetuating traditional disciplinary assumptions. "Reconceptualization of knowledge is central to a gender-balanced transformation of the curriculum. Reconceptualization necessitates the critical practice of questioning the assumptions, categories, and paradigms that have dominated the definition and production of knowledge" (Franzosa and Mazza 1984, p. xi). Both gender and ethnic studies programs have an ideological aspect, a desire to foster paradigm change in the liberal arts curriculum through greater emphasis on the role of women, blacks, and other minority groups (Schuster and Van Dyne 1984, p. 59). Gender has become an important variable in social science research, leading to critiques of traditional theories, methodologies, and scholarship, the formulation of new theoretical models, and pressure to "legitimize interdisciplinary work" (Boroviak 1984, p. 42).

Three primary models have dominated efforts to transform the curriculum in over 50 women's studies projects initiated with federal or foundation funding: (1) top-down transformation initiated by administrative directive to integrate introductory women's studies courses into existing departments; (2) piggyback transformation, in which existing interdisciplinary courses and programs are targeted as the best way to begin change in the curriculum; and (3) bottom-up transformation that originates with faculty whose research and teaching are focused on a particular topic (Schuster and Van Dyne 1984, p. 65). Mainstreaming projects tend to minimize women's studies programs, and "effective transformation will not occur without a base of researchers and teachers whose primary concern is women" (p. 63).

Ethnic studies programs combine courses in language, social or regional dialects, or literature with work in sociology, anthropology, history, or related fields (MLA 1986a). Some examples are black studies, Chicano studies, third world studies, Asian-American studies, American Indian studies, and Puerto Rican studies.

The Master of Arts in Liberal Studies (M.A.L.S.) offers students the opportunity to undertake multidisciplinary study in the arts, humanities, and natural and social sciences. Content of courses is innovative, and programs often have distinctive themes. The first M.A.L.S. was offered at Wesleyan University in 1952 as a summer program for teachers. It is particularly suitable for master's level universities in which graduate research is not the first priority, the majority of graduate students attend part time, the faculty are practitioner oriented, course work is emphasized more than research, and the liberal arts and science departments are well established and generally seeking students. It has given graduate faculty the opportunity to develop innovative courses oriented toward problems in a field.

The M.A. in designated concentrations is a variation on the M.A.L.S. Iowa State University offers a general graduate studies program leading to an M.A. in five concentrations—the arts and humanities, biological science, physical science, social science, and international development. Students take 35 credits in at least three of the five fields chosen from 26 academic departments and interdisciplinary programs. The College of Engineering of the University of California at Berkeley has its own dean of interdisciplinary studies and offers a two-year Master of Engineering in the applications of technical, social, and economic knowledge to the analysis and solution of engineering problems leading to degrees in bioengineering, earthquake engineering, energy resources, ocean engineering, and urban and public systems (Rader 1982).

In restructuring the master's degree to encourage inter- and multidisciplinary study, faculty have incorporated such innovations as field-based internships, self-directed study, and distance learning. While traditional degree structures dominate, evidence suggests that educational technology in particular will have a considerable impact on the organization and curriculum of professional degree programs. The potential graduate student population is now older, changes careers more often, and is interested in programs that are flexible, accessible, and responsive to its needs.

External degrees and experiential learning are two approaches that articulate the learning needs of adults. They combine theory with practice, emphasizing self-directed study and individualized programs (Jacobs and Allen 1982, p. 1). Empire State College, the State University of New York's external degree college, offers three related M.A. degree programs in policy studies in business, labor, and culture. Brief residencies are combined with longer periods of directed independent study, individual contract learning, cross-registration with other SUNY campuses, supervised internships, or other means of study approved by the student's academic advisory panel and under the guidance of a faculty mentor. All three of these M.A. programs require 36 credits of graduate study culminating in a comprehensive examination and a final project in the form of a thesis, field research, or practicum involving an in-depth policy study.

Cooperative education originated at Antioch College, which offers 33 master's degrees at six campuses, combining interdisciplinary course work with field-based internships and independent research (Rader 1982). The cooperative experience offers graduate credit for supervised internships and has become common in fields ranging from arts administration to psychiatric social work and health care management. It is now an important part of professional degree programs and in several fields is a requirement for permanent licensing.

State universities and interuniversity consortia are exploring innovative delivery systems—computer networks, interactive telecommunications, and satellite television receivers. The University of South Carolina offers a part-time, 63-credit M.B.A. for students employed full time. It combines graduate courses with televised sessions at regional technical educational centers around the state. Courses are transmitted on closed-circuit facilities by the South Carolina Educational Television Network, and direct contact between students and faculty occurs through interactive telecommunication links. The potential uses of educational technology are only now beginning to be understood, and as costs are reduced and faculty become more adept at using computers, videodiscs, and other innovative teaching tools, they will be integrated into master's level programs and will accelerate the process of change.

Consortia among colleges and universities located geographically close to each other or linked through computer networks have been organized as a cost-effective means to share resources and reduce duplication (Glazer 1982). The Western Interstate Commission for Higher Education (WICHE) and the Southern Regional Education Board (SREB) publish inventories of master's degrees that are offered cooperatively to students in their respective regions at tuition rates for residents. WICHE offers 76 master's degree programs to students in 30 graduate-level universities in 12 western states and in 1985 initiated regional arrangements among five northwestern states in 31 master's degree programs that are considered of high quality and distinctive and are selected through a competitive process (WICHE 1985). The SREB Academic Common Market is an arrangement among 13 southern states that allows participating students to pay in-state tuition while studying outside their home states. More than 1,000 master's programs are available through the plan. Consortial arrangements and regional compacts are two structural innovations that permit the sharing of institutional resources through a variety of mechanisms, including joint faculty appointments, cross-registration, and collaborative planning of new programs (Glazer 1982, pp. 183–85).

CONCLUSIONS

The master's degree is diverse, it is traditional, and it is professional. A new paradigm of this degree has evolved in the United States, partly a function of an egalitarian system of postsecondary education that has provided universal access regardless of financial need or academic ability. In a society like ours that honors credentials, the master's degree has come to signify professionalism across many disciplines and specializations. The dominant paradigm is practitioner oriented, emphasizing training in skills, career development, and pragmatic goals. It is linked to the needs of the student and the demands of the marketplace and driven by externally imposed standards, and it emphasizes practice rather than theory, skills rather than research, training rather than scholarship—which does not imply that those who seek these degrees are less academic, less intellectual, or less prepared in the liberal arts than their peers in graduate arts and science programs. They are, however, seeking skills that will prepare them for the work force.

. . . It emphasizes practice rather than theory, skills rather than research, training rather than scholarship.

The problems are overlapping and relate to the paradigmatic shift from the arts and science model to manifold professional degrees. This shift has occurred within the past two decades as public policy has influenced the expansion of higher education and the involvement of government in social problems, and as women and minorities have gained access to spheres of business and management previously closed. The following salient issues, identified in reviewing the literature and in talking with educators, policy makers, and professionals, constitute an attempt to devise an organizing framework through which to better understand this degree.

1. *The Master of Arts and Master of Science are of doubtful utility in arts and science doctoral programs.* While the M.A. could be strengthened by mandating that everyone obtain an intermediate degree before completing requirements for the Ph.D. (Spurr 1970) and while the need for links between professional and graduate schools is apparent (Pelikan 1983), the 30- to 32-credit M.A. or M.S. is not necessarily relevant for the doctoral student. The original purpose of the master's degree was to provide the postbaccalaureate with a second credential from his alma mater, one that would be of particular

use in divinity and subsequently in secondary school teaching. As the first year of graduate study, it has little meaning. As a consolation prize, it has even less. Further discussion is warranted as to its purpose in graduate programs leading to the Ph.D.

2. *The master's degree is overwhelmingly professional, it is largely terminal, and it is practice oriented.* As a professional degree, it is aligned closely with specialized accreditation agencies, professional associations, and potential employers. Master's programs typically balance these interests with the missions and purposes of the college or university that grants them, which has implications for the way they are administered, staffed, and supported, for the population they serve, and for the outcomes they seek to achieve. Underlying these factors are their diversity, quality, and integrity in the academic community.

3. *The lack of economic analysis of the master's degree is striking.* Oblique references have been made to the cost-benefit advantages of the degree, but they are not reinforced by any data. Financial analyses quantify data on enrollments, degrees conferred, and in some fields on employment outcomes. Assumptions are made that master's degrees make money or conversely that they are costly and inefficient, but data are not readily available for faculty salaries, tuition income, program costs, and ancillary resources that support master's degrees. The kinds of studies that the National Board of Graduate Education undertook (1975) or that Cartter conducted of the academic labor market (1976) have not been extrapolated to professional degrees except the M.B.A. and in science and engineering. Some assessments are needed of the costs of proliferation, specialization, and diversity within and among professional master's degrees.

4. *Quality control is problematic.* Accreditation, state oversight, and the activities of professional associations attempt to set the standards and to define the parameters for program design, implementation, and evaluation. New degrees and new specializations are largely within the purview of the institution, however, and where a need is perceived, a program is ready to meet it. The

Graduate Program Self-Assessment Service is one effort
to devise a mechanism for assessing master's programs,
but as a voluntary process with meticulous attention to
detail, it is apt to be threatening to marginal departments, programs, or institutions. More work is needed in
designing and carrying out quality control. Faculty productivity is not the only measure of quality in professional master's degrees. They are not research degrees
but degrees oriented toward practice rather than theory.
They require proficient teachers skilled in new technologies and cognizant of the environment in which students
seek to fulfill professional goals; as such, the emphasis
on scholarly productivity may be irrelevant as a measure
of a program's quality.

5. *Diversity and proliferation have engendered ambigu-
ity in the meaning of the master's degree.* For the past
85 years, academics have been critical of the inability of
institutions of higher education to check the proliferation
of the master's degree. Many attempts have been made
to codify the degree, to rein it in through various mechanisms, and to eliminate duplicative, unproductive programs. Despite these admonitions, diversification continues unabated, as evidenced by the Office of Educational
Research and Improvement's new taxonomy of degrees
recently adopted for reporting purposes (OERI 1985). At
the master's level, 633 degrees are designated in 30 disciplines; with combined degrees the possible combinations
total almost 800. The relationship of the master's degree
to the baccalaureate and the doctorate has become am-
biguous in the hierarchy of academic degrees. An in-
depth assessment should be undertaken to address problems of proliferation and to clarify the meaning of the
master's degree.

6. *The needs of part-time, adult populations and mixed
cohorts are not being addressed adequately in master's
degree programs.* The literature on innovation is sparse,
and those programs that are offered through flexible
scheduling, concentrated time frames, self-paced study,
experiential learning, technology-based delivery systems, and student-mentor relationships are few and far

between. We continue to impose the same traditional credit-based classroom model upon both mid-career and 22-year-old postbaccalaureate students, to adhere to standardized test scores and cumulative grade point averages as the twin predictors of academic success in professional degree programs, to provide few services to commuting full-time employed students, and to treat adult students as consumers rather than producers of knowledge. As a result, corporations, school systems, and other noncollegiate institutions have set up parallel professional development courses and degrees (Eurich 1985).

7. *At issue today are the expectations shared by faculty in designing new programs or strengthening existing ones.* The level of difficulty and what constitutes a graduate course are aspects of the problem being aired in conjunction with external evaluations. Institutional policies and practices need to be reviewed with respect to graduate students' earning credits for basic rather than advanced courses, particularly when the undergraduate degree is in an unrelated field. The prevalence of this problem runs counter to the original design of the master's degree as a fifth-year, postbaccalaureate certificate to expand and strengthen knowledge and skills in the undergraduate major. In this context, we must also examine policies with regard to undergraduates enrolled in graduate-level courses, granting credit for previous learning, life experience, proficiency examinations, continuing education credits, and other options. The adaptation of different curricular models to meet guidelines of the department, college, university, accrediting agency, or, in some cases, the external contractor of university services has made comparability a frustrating exercise. Every model that is designed seems to have several exceptions, thus adding to the complexity, diversity, and inability to standardize various master's degree curricula. Although certain first professional degrees have managed to retain a single designation—that is, the M.B.A., the J.D., the M.D.—specialized master's degrees are offered following the J.D. and the M.D. (OERI 1985; Ruud 1985), and in the case of the M.B.A.,

M.S. degrees with qualifying phrases are alternative options (Hugstad 1983).

A concerted effort is needed to focus on the master's degree—its economics, its academic strengths and weaknesses, its diffuse character, and its importance in the hierarchy of degrees. To do so, it is incumbent upon us to recognize that the master's degree is distinct from other graduate degrees and that it is a class of degrees rather than one generic model. By addressing the issues pervading this degree, we can modify and adapt a variety of models that will enhance and strengthen postbaccalaureate education.

APPENDIX A

ABBREVIATIONS

AACN	American Association of Colleges of Nursing
AACSB	American Assembly of Collegiate Schools of Business
AACTE	American Association of Colleges of Teacher Education
AALS	American Association of Library Schools
AASSW	American Association of Schools of Social Work
AAU	Association of American Universities
ABA	American Bar Association
ABET	Accreditation Board for Engineering and Technology
ACE	American Council on Education
ACEJMC	Accrediting Council on Education in Journalism and Mass Communications
AGS	Association of Graduate Schools
ALA	American Library Association
AMCEE	Association for Media-based Continuing Education for Engineers
ANA	American Nursing Association
ASEE	American Society for Engineering Education
AUPHA	Association of University Programs in Health Administration
BEL	Board of Education for Librarianship
CGS	Council of Graduate Schools in the United States
COPA	Council on Postsecondary Accreditation
CORE	Commission on Rehabilitation Education
CRCC	Commission on Rehabilitation Counseling Certification
CSWE	Council on Social Work Education
ETS	Educational Testing Service
GMAC	Graduate Management Admissions Council
GMAT	Graduate Management Admissions Test
GPSA	Graduate Program Self-Assessment Service
GREB	Graduate Record Examination Board
HEADS	Higher Education Arts Data Services
MLA	Modern Language Association
NASAD	National Association of Schools of Art and Design
NASD	National Association of Schools of Dance
NASM	National Association of Schools of Music
NASPAA	National Association of Schools of Public Affairs and Administration
NAST	National Association of Schools of Theatre
NASW	National Association of Social Workers
NBGE	National Board of Graduate Education

NCATE	National Council for Accreditation of Teacher Education
NCES	National Center for Education Statistics
NIH	National Institutes of Health
NLN	National League of Nursing
NSF	National Science Foundation
OERI	Office of Educational Research and Improvement
SREB	Southern Regional Education Board
WICHE	Western Interstate Commission for Higher Education

APPENDIX B

DEGREES

The following degrees are discussed in this study. They are only a partial list of the hundreds of degrees offered by colleges and universities in the United States.

A.A.	Associate of Arts
B.A.	Bachelor of Arts
B.L.S.	Bachelor of Library Science
B.S.	Bachelor of Science
B.S.N.	Bachelor of Science in Nursing
B.S.W.	Bachelor of Social Work
C.A.S.	Certificate of Advanced Study
D.A.	Doctor of Arts
D.P.A.	Doctor of Public Administration
D.S.W.	Doctor of Social Work
Ed.D.	Doctor of Education
J.D.	Juris Doctor
LL.B.	Bachelor of Laws
LL.M.	Master of Laws
M.A.	Master of Arts
M.A.L.D.	Master of Arts in Law and Diplomacy
M.A.L.I.R.	Master of Law in Labor and Industrial Relations
M.A.L.S.	Master of Arts in Liberal Studies; Master of Asian Law
M.A.T.	Master of Arts in Teaching
M.B.A.	Master of Business Administration
M.C.J.	Master of Comparative Jurisprudence
M.C.L.	Master of Comparative Law
M.D.	Doctor of Medicine
M.E.	Master of Engineering
M.Ed.	Master of Education
M.Eng.	Master of Engineering
M.F.A.	Master of Fine Arts
M.H.A.	Master of Health Administration
M.H.P.M.	Master of Health Policy and Management
M.H.S.A.	Master of Health Services Administration
M.L.I.	Master of Arts or Science in Legal Institutions
M.L.I.S.	Master of Law in Information Science
M.L.S.	Master of Library Science
M.M.	Master of Management; Master of Music
M.M.E.	Master of Mechanical Engineering
M.M.P.A.	Master of Municipal Public Administration
M.N.	Master of Nursing
M.P.A.	Master of Public Administration
M.P.H.	Master of Public Health
M.Phil.	Master of Philosophy

M.P.L.	Master of Urban Planning
M.P.P.	Master of Public Policy
M.S.	Master of Science
M.S.G.	Master of Science in Gerontology
M.S.I.M.	Master of Science in Industrial Management
M.S.I.S.	Master of Science in Information Science
M.S.M.	Master of Science in Management
M.S.N.	Master of Science in Nursing
M.S.W.	Master of Social Work
M.U.A.	Master of Urban Affairs
Ph.D.	Doctor of Philosophy
R.N.	Registered Nurse
S.J.D.	Doctor of Juridical Science

REFERENCES

The ERIC Clearinghouse on Higher Education abstracts and indexes the current literature on higher education for the Office of Educational Research and Improvement's monthly bibliographic journal, *Resources in Education*. Most of these publications are available through the ERIC Document Reproduction Service (EDRS). For publications cited in this bibliography that are available from EDRS, ordering number and price are included. Readers who wish to order a publication should write to the ERIC Document Reproduction Service, 3900 Wheeler Avenue, Alexandria, Virginia 22304. When ordering, please specify the document number. Documents are available as noted in microfiche (MF) and paper copy (PC). Because prices are subject to change, it is advisable to check the latest issue of *Resources in Education* for current cost based on the number of pages in the publication.

Accreditation Board for Engineering and Technology. October 1984. *Proposed Revision of Criteria for Accrediting Programs in Engineering in the United States*. New York: Author.

———. 1985. *Annual Report*. New York: Author.

Adkins, Douglas L. 1971. *The Great American Degree Machine: An Economic Analysis of the Human Resource Output of Higher Education*. Berkeley, Cal.: Carnegie Foundation for the Advancement of Teaching.

Albrecht, Paul A. 1984. "Opportunity and Impediment in Graduate Program Innovation." In *Keeping Graduate Programs Responsive to National Needs*, edited by M. Pelczar and L. Solmon. New Directions in Higher Education No. 46. San Francisco: Jossey-Bass.

American Assembly of Collegiate Schools of Business. 1984–85. *Accreditation Council Policies, Procedures, and Standards, 1984–85*. St. Louis: Author.

———. February 1986. *Newsline* 16:1.

American Association of Colleges of Nursing. 1985. *Directory*. Washington, D.C.: Author.

American Association of Colleges of Teacher Education. 1983. *Report to the Profession, 1982*. Washington, D.C.: Author.

———. July 1984. "1984 Report to the Profession: Data Show Innovation, Change." *Briefs* 5: 1–11.

American Association for Engineering Societies. April 1985. "Engineering and Technology Degrees, 1984." *Engineering Education* 75: 637–45.

American Bar Association. 1984. *A Review of Legal Education in the United States, Fall 1983: Law Schools and Bar Admission Requirements*. Chicago: ABA, Section of Legal Education and Admissions to the Bar.

APWA/NASPAA Joint Committee on Education for Public Works/Environmental Administration. 1983. "Guidelines for Developing a Master's Degree Specialization in Public Works Administration within the M.P.A. Degree." Washington, D.C.: National Association of Schools of Public Affairs and Administration.

Association of American Universities. 1910. "The Degree of Master of Arts." *Journal of Proceedings and Addresses* 12: 34–50.

———. 1927. " 'Debunking' the Master's Degree." *Journal of Proceedings and Addresses* 29: 108–11.

———. 1935. "Problems of the Master's Degree." *Journal of Proceedings and Addresses* 35: 32–37.

———. 1945. "The Master's Degree." *Journal of Proceedings and Addresses* 46: 111–25.

Atkin, J. Myron. 1983. "American Graduate Schools of Education: A View from Abroad." *Oxford Review of Education* 9: 63–70.

Azzara, Frank. 1985."Comparative Analysis of 15 Metropolitan Area M.B.A. Programs." Unpublished data. New York:St. John's University.

Baker, Richard T. 1954. *A History of the Graduate School of Journalism*. New York: Columbia University Press.

Balint, Jane; Menninger, Kathleen; and Hurt, Melanie. March/ April 1983. "Job Opportunities for Master's Prepared Nurses." *Nursing Outlook* 31: 109–14.

Berelson, Bernard. 1960. *Graduate Education in the United States*. New York: McGraw-Hill.

———, ed. 1970. *Education for Librarianship*. Reprint. Freeport, N.Y.: Books for Libraries Press.

Berg, Helen, and Ferber, Marianne. December 1983. "Men and Women Graduate Students: Who Succeeds and Why?" *Journal of Higher Education* 54: 639–48.

Berryman, Sue; Langer, Paul; Pincus, John; and Soloman, Richard. 1979. *Foreign Language and International Studies Specialists: The Marketplace and National Policy*. Santa Monica, Cal.: Rand Corp. ED 188 446. 261 pp. MF–$1.00; PC–$23.34.

Birnbaum, Robert. 1983. *Maintaining Diversity in Higher Education*. San Francisco: Jossey-Bass.

Blau, Peter M., and Margulies, Rebecca. 1973. "The Reputations of American Professional Schools." *Change* 6: 42–47.

Blegen, Theodore. March 1959. "How Can Graduate Schools Increase the Supply of College Teachers?" *Journal of Higher Education* 30: 127–33.

Bok, Derek. 1982. *Beyond the Ivory Tower: Social Responsibilities of the Modern University.* Cambridge, Mass.: Harvard University Press.

Born, Catherine. Fall 1982. "Coping with an Environment of Scarcity: Graduate Social Work Programs and Responses to the Current Crises." *Journal of Education for Social Work* 18: 5–13.

Boroviak, Darlene L. 1984. "The Social Sciences: Establishing Gender as a Category." In *Toward a Balanced Curriculum: A Sourcebook for Initiating Gender Integration Projects,* edited by B. Spanier, A. Bloom, and D. Boroviak. Cambridge, Mass.: Schenkman Publishing Co.

Bowen, Howard R., and Schuster, Jack H. 1986. *American Professors: A National Resource Imperiled.* New York: Oxford University Press.

Brademas, John. 1983. *Signs of Trouble and Erosion: A Report on Graduate Education in America.* Washington, D.C.: National Commission on Student Financial Assistance. ED 239 546. 87 pp. MF–$1.00; PC–$9.56.

Bureau of College Evaluation. 1972. *Master's Degrees in the State of New York, 1969–70.* Albany: State Education Department.

Cameron, Catherine. 1984. "Task Force on Instruction Improvement Summary of Data on Master's Degree Programs." Washington, D.C.: American Association for Adult and Continuing Education, Commission of Professors of Education. ED 244 103. 12 pp. MF–$1.00; PC–$3.59.

Carbino, Rosemarie, and Morgenbesser, Mel. Fall 1982. "A National Challenge: The Decline in M.S.W. Admissions Applications." *Journal of Social Work Education* 18: 13–22.

Carmichael, Oliver. 1960. "A Three-Year Master's Degree Beginning with the Junior Year in College." *Journal of Higher Education* 31: 162–77.

———. 1961. *Graduate Education: A Critique and a Program.* New York: Harper & Row.

Carnegie Forum Task Force on Teaching as a Profession. 1986. *A Nation Prepared: Teachers for the 21st Century.* Hyattsville, Md.: Carnegie Forum on Education and the Economy.

Cartter, A. A. 1966. *An Assessment of Quality in Graduate Education.* Washington, D.C.: American Council on Education.

Cartter, A. A., and Solmon, L. C. February 1977. "The Cartter Report on the Leading Schools of Education, Law, and Business." *Change* 9: 44–48.

Cartter, Alan. 1976. *Ph.D.s and the Academic Labor Market.* New York: McGraw-Hill.

Clark, Ann. 1980. "Adult Development and the Experience of
Graduate Education." Washington, D.C.: National Institute of
Education. ED 197 067. 78 pp. MF–$1.00; PC–$9.56.

Clark, Mary Jo, and Hartnett, Rodney T. 1977. *The Assessment
of Quality in Graduate Education: Summary of a Multidimensional Approach.* Washington, D.C.: Council of Graduate
Schools in the United States.

Clark, Mary Jo; Hartnett, Rodney T.; and Baird, Leonard L.
1976. "Assessing Dimensions of Quality in Doctoral Education:
A Technical Report of a National Study in Three Fields."
Princeton, N.J.: Educational Testing Service. ED 173 144.
427 pp. MF–$1.00; PC–$36.29.

Coley, Richard J., and Thorpe, Margaret E. 1986. *A Look at the
M.A.T. Model of Teacher Education and Its Graduates: Les-
sons for Today.* Princeton, N.J.: Educational Testing Service.
ED 272 457. 94 pp. MF–$1.00; PC–$9.14.

Collins, Randall. 1979. *The Credential Society: An Historical
Sociology of Education and Stratification.* New York: Academic Press.

Commission on Rehabilitation Counselor Certification. July 1984.
Guide to Rehabilitation Counselor Certification. Arlington
Heights, Ill.: Author.

Conant, Ralph W. 1980. *The Conant Report: A Study of the Education of Librarians.* Cambridge, Mass.: MIT Press.

Conrad, Clifton F., and Blackburn, Robert T. 1985a. "Correlates
of Departmental Quality in Regional Colleges and Universities." *American Educational Research Journal* 22: 279–95.

———. 1985b. "Program Quality in Higher Education: A Review
and Critique of Literature and Research." *Higher Education:
Handbook of Theory and Research,* vol. 1, edited by J. C.
Smart. New York: Agathon Press.

Cremin, Lawrence A. 1983. "The Problematics of Education in
the 1980s: Some Reflections on the Oxford Workshop." *Oxford
Review of Education* 9: 9–20.

Council of Graduate Schools in the United States. 1963. Proceedings of Annual Meeting. Washington, D.C.: Author.

———. 1966. "The Master's Degree." Washington, D.C.:
Author.

———. 1970. Proceedings of Annual Meeting. Washington, D.C.:
Author.

———. 1972. Proceedings of Annual Meeting. Washington, D.C.:
Author.

———. 1975. Proceedings of Annual Meeting. Washington, D.C.:
Author.

———. 1976. *The Master's Degree: A Policy Statement.* Washington, D.C.: Author. ED 153 588. 17 pp. MF–$1.00; PC–$3.59.

———. 1977. Proceedings of Annual Meeting. Washington, D.C.: Author.

———. 1979. "The Assessment of Quality in Master's Programs." *Proceedings*. College Park: University of Maryland. ED 196 960. 195 pp. MF–$1.00; PC–$16.96.

———. 1981. Proceedings of Annual Meeting. Washington, D.C.: Author.

———. 1982a. Proceedings of Annual Meeting. Washington, D.C.: Author.

———. 1982b. "Recent Developments in Graduate Programs. New Opportunities through Versatility: Broadening the Mold." *Proceedings of Conference of CGS/GREB*. ED 234 660. 198 pp. MF–$1.00; PC–$16.96.

———. 1983. "Graduate Education—New Connections." *Proceedings of the Annual Meeting of the Council of Graduate Schools in the United States,* edited by E. M. Khalil. Washington, D.C.: Author. ED 253 175. 125 pp. MF–$1.00; PC–$11.41.

Council of Graduate Schools/National Science Foundation. 1980. *Industry/University Cooperative Programs*. Proceedings of a workshop held in conjunction with the 20th annual meeting of the Council of Graduate Schools in the U.S. Washington, D.C.: Council of Graduate Schools. ED 215 612. 127 pp. MF–$1.00; PC–$10.99.

Council on Postsecondary Accreditation. July 1984. *The Balance Wheel for Accreditation*. Washington, D.C.: Author.

Danton, J. Periam. Fall 1983. "Notes on the Evaluation of Library Schools." *Journal of Education for Librarianship* 24: 106–16.

Darling, Richard L. 1980. "Two-Year Master's Programs in Library Education: A Conference Call." In *Extended Library Education Programs,* edited by R. L. Darling and T. Belanger. New York: Columbia University, School of Library Science.

Darling, Richard L., and Belanger, Terry, eds. 1980. *Extended Library Education Programs*. New York: Columbia University, School of Library Science.

Dewey, Barbara I. May/June 1985. "Dual Degree Programs: Indiana University's Experience." *Catholic Library World* 56: 430–33.

Dieter, G. E. 1984. "Graduate Education in Engineering." In *Keeping Graduate Programs Responsive to National Needs,* edited by M. Pelczar and L. Solmon. New Directions in Higher Education No. 46. San Francisco: Jossey-Bass.

Dinerman, Miriam. Spring 1982. "Study of Baccalaureate and Master's Curricula in Social Work." *Journal of Social Work Education* 18: 84–92.

Dinerman, Miriam, and Geismar, Ludwig L., eds. 1984. *A Quarter Century of Social Work Education.* New York: National Association of Social Workers and Council on Social Work Education.

Doignan, Paul. April 1985. "Engineering and Engineering Technology Degrees Granted, 1984." *Engineering Education* 75: 637–45.

Downey, B. J. 1979. "What Is the Assessment of Quality in Master's Programs?" In *The Assessment of Quality in Master's Programs,* edited by the Council of Graduate Schools. College Park: University of Maryland. ED 196 960. 195 pp. MF–$1.00; PC–$16.96.

Dressel, Paul L. 1960. *Liberal Education and Journalism.* New York: Teachers College, Institute of Higher Education. ED 217 750. 33 pp. MF–$1.00; PC–$5.44.

———. 1978. "Problems and Principles in the Recognition or Accreditation of Graduate Education." Report no. 4 of the Project to Develop Evaluative Criteria and Procedures for the Accreditation of Nontraditional Education, vol. 3. Washington, D.C.: Council on Postsecondary Education. ED 165 568. 51 pp. MF–$1.00; PC–$7.29.

———. 1982. *College Teaching as a Profession: The Doctor of Arts Degree.* Washington, D.C.: Council of Graduate Schools in the United States.

Earley, Penelope. 1985. *Teacher Education Policy in the States: 50-State Survey of Legislative and Administrative Actions.* Washington, D.C.: American Association of Colleges of Teacher Education. ED 257 833. 85 pp. MF–$1.00; PC–$9.56.

Eels, Walter Crosby. 1963. *Degrees in Higher Education.* Washington, D.C.: The Center for Applied Research in Education.

Eels, Walter C., and Haswell, Harold A. 1960. *Academic Degrees: Earned and Honorary Degrees Conferred by Institutions of Higher Education in the United States.* No. 28. Washington, D.C.: U.S. Office of Education.

Elder, J. P. March 1959. "Reviving the Master's Degree for the Prospective College Teacher." *Journal of Higher Education* 30: 133–36.

Ellis, R. A. November 1985. "Engineering Enrollments, Fall 1984." *Engineering Education* 75: 102–8.

Engineering Foundation and ABET. 1982. *Engineering Education: Aims and Goals for the Eighties.* New York: Accreditation Board for Engineering and Technology.

Erdman, R. L. 1979. "Graduate Programs in Education: Past, Present, and Future." In *Perspectives on Graduate Programs in Education,* edited by L. Pipes. Washington, D.C.: AACTE. ED 173 277. 122 pp. MF–$1.00; PC–$11.41.

Eurich, Nell P. 1985. *Corporate Classrooms: The Learning Business*. Lawrenceville, N.J.: Princeton University Press.

Ewalt, Patricia L. 1983. *Curriculum Design and Development for Graduate Social Work Education*. New York: Council on Social Work Education.

Eyler, Janet. 1984. "The Politics of Quality in Higher Education." In *Financial Incentives for Academic Quality*, edited by J. Folger. New Directions for Higher Education No. 48. San Francisco: Jossey-Bass.

Feistritzer, C. Emily. 1983. *The Condition of Teaching: A State-by-State Analysis*. Princeton, N.J.: Carnegie Foundation for the Advancement of Teaching.

———. 1984. *The Making of a Teacher: A Report on Teacher Education and Certification*. Washington, D.C.: National Center for Educational Information.

Filerman, Gary L. 1981. "Varieties of Health Administrator Education." In *The Challenge of Administering Health Services: Career Pathways*, edited by L. E. Bellin and L. E. Weeks. Washington, D.C.: AUPHA Press.

Flexner, Abraham. 1930. *Universities: American, English, German*. New York: Oxford University Press.

Florida State Board of Education. 1982. *The Master Plan for Florida Postsecondary Education*. Tallahassee: Florida State Board of Education Postsecondary Planning Commission.

Folger, John, ed. 1984. *Financial Incentives for Academic Quality*. New Directions for Higher Education No. 48. San Francisco: Jossey-Bass.

Franzosa, Susan D., and Mazza, Karen A. 1984. *Integrating Women's Studies into the Curriculum: An Annotated Bibliography*. Westport, Conn.: Greenwood Press.

Gerald, Debra E., ed. 1985. *Projections of Education Statistics to 1992–93*. Washington, D.C.: National Center for Education Statistics.

Giametti, A. Bartlett. 1981. *The University and the Public Interest*. New York: Atheneum.

Glazer, Judith S. 1982. "Designing and Managing an Inter-university Consortium in a Period of Decline." *Journal of Higher Education* 53: 177–94.

Gleaves, Edwin S. Spring 1982. "Library Education: Issues for the Eighties." *Journal of Education for Librarianship* 22: 260–74.

Goertz, Margaret E. January 1986. *State Educational Standards: A 50-State Survey*. Princeton, N.J.: Educational Testing Service.

Goldstein, Amy J., and Frary, Andrea C., eds. 1985. *Graduate and Professional Programs: An Overview 1986*. Book 1, 20th ed. Princeton, N.J.: Peterson's Annual Guides/Graduate Study.

Golladay, Mary A. 1983. "Graduate Study in Education: An Analysis of Institutions and Degree Awards, 1971–1981." ED 240 064. 28 pp. MF–$1.00; PC–$5.44.

Gordon, Robert, and Howell, James. 1959. *Higher Education for Business*. New York: Columbia University Press.

Graduate Program Self-Assessment Service. 1983. *GPSA Specimen Kit for Master's Level Programs*. Princeton, N.J.: Educational Testing Service.

Grant, W. Vance, and Snyder, Thomas, eds. 1983. *Digest of Educational Statistics, 1983–1984*. Washington, D.C.: National Center for Education Statistics.

Gurin, Arnold, and Williams, David. 1973. "Social Work Education." In *Education for the Professions of Medicine, Law, Theology, and Social Welfare*, edited by E. Hughes. New York: McGraw-Hill.

Harcleroad, Fred F. 1980. *Accreditation: History, Process, and Problems*. AAHE-ERIC Higher Education Research Report No. 6. Washington, D.C.: American Association for Higher Education. ED 198 774. 60 pp. MF–$1.00; PC–$7.29.

Hart, Sylvia E. 1981. "Generic Graduate Programs in Nursing." In *Graduate Education in Nursing: Issues and Future Directions*, edited by M. H. Smith. Atlanta: Southern Regional Education Board. ED 210 972. 59 pp. MF–$1.00; PC–$7.29.

Hartman, Ann. Spring 1983. "Concentrations, Specializations, and Curriculum Design in M.S.W. and B.S.W. Programs." *Journal of Education for Social Work* 19: 18–27.

Harvard University School of Public Health. 1978. "Review, Evaluation, and Modification of the Educational Program of the Harvard School of Public Health." Washington, D.C.: Health Resources Administration. ED 165 699. 92 pp. MF–$1.00; PC–$9.14.

Hathaway, Baxter. 1975. "The M.F.A. and the University." *Associated Writing Programs: 1975 Catalogue of Programs*. Reprint: Chestertown, Md.

Hauptman, Arthur M. 1986. *Students in Graduate and Professional Education: What We Know and Need to Know*. Washington, D.C.: Association of American Universities.

Hayes, Robert M. 1980. "The UCLA Experience with the M.L.S." In *Extended Library Education Programs*, edited by R. L. Darling and T. Belanger. New York: Columbia University, School of Library Science.

Hennessey, John W., Jr. Autumn 1984. "Continuity and Change: M.B.A. Students 1954–1984." *Selections* 1: 23–27.

Higher Education Arts Data Services. 1985. *Data Summary, 1983–1984: Art/Design; Dance; Music; Theatre*. Reston, Va.: National Association of Schools of Art and Design; National Association of Schools of Dance; National Association of Schools of Music; National Association of Schools of Theatre; International Council of Fine Arts Deans.

Holmes Group. 1986. *Tomorrow's Teachers: A Report of the Holmes Group*. East Lansing, Mich.: Author.

Hoot, James L. 1983. "Improving the Education of Very Young Children and Boosting University Enrollment through a Master's Degree Program in Child Care Administration." ED 242 424. 18 pp. MF–$1.00; PC–$3.59.

Howard, Maureen. 25 May 1986. "Can Writing Be Taught in Iowa?" *New York Times Magazine* 135: 34–36 + .

Hughes, Everett, ed. 1973. *Education for the Professions of Medicine, Law, Theology, and Social Welfare*. New York: McGraw-Hill.

Hugstad, Paul S. 1983. *The Business School in the 1980s: Liberalism versus Vocationalism*. New York: Praeger.

Humphreys, Nancy, and Dinerman, Miriam. 1984. "Professionalizing Social Work." In *A Quarter Century of Social Work Education*, edited by M. Dinerman and L. L. Geismar. New York: National Association of Social Workers and Council on Social Work Education.

Hunger, J. David, and Wheelen, Thomas L. 1980a. "A Performance Appraisal of Undergraduate Business Education." *Human Resource Management* 19: 24–31.

———. Fall 1980b. "A Recruiter's Question: How Does the Bachelor's Degree in Business Compare to the M.B.A.?" *Sloan Management Review* 19: 2–7.

Huston, Jeffrey C., and Burnet, George. January 1984. "What One Thousand Seniors Think of Graduate Study." *Engineering Education* 74: 221–24.

Hutchins, Robert M. 1936. *The Higher Learning in America*. New Haven, Conn.: Yale University Press.

Jacobs, Frederic, and Allen, Richard J., eds. 1982. *Expanding the Missions of Graduate and Professional Education*. New Directions in Experiential Learning No. 10. San Francisco: Jossey-Bass.

Jenkins, Roger; Reizenstein, Richard; and Rodgers, F. G. September/October 1984. "Report Cards on the M.B.A." *Harvard Business Review* 62: 20–30.

Johnson, Jenny K. September 1985. "A Matter of Degrees." *Tech Trends* 30: 27–28.

Jones, L. V.; Lindzey, G.; and Coggeshall, P. E., eds. 1982. *An Assessment of Research—Doctorate Programs in the United States*. 5 vol. Washington, D.C.: National Academy Press.

Judge, Harry. 1982. *American Graduate Schools of Education: A View from Abroad*. New York: Ford Foundation.

Kelley, Jean. 1981. "Purposes of Graduate Education: An Evaluation." In *Graduate Education in Nursing: Issues and Future Directions,* edited by M. Smith. Atlanta: Southern Regional Education Board. ED 210 972. 59 pp. MF–$1.00; PC–$7.29.

Kiechel, Walter, III. 18 June 1979. "Harvard Business School Restudies Itself." *Fortune* 99: 48–58.

Kirkwood, Robert. Summer 1985. "The Quest for Quality in Graduate Education." *Educational Record* 66: 4–9.

Kuh, George D. 1981. *Indices of Quality in the Undergraduate Experience*. AAHE-ERIC Higher Education Research Report No. 4. Washington, D.C.: American Association for Higher Education. ED 213 340. 50 pp. MF–$1.00; PC–$5.44.

Kurst, Charlotte, ed. 1984. *The Official Guide to M.B.A. Programs, Admissions, and Careers*. Princeton, N.J.: Educational Testing Service, Graduate Management Admissions Council.

Lane, Marcia S., ed. 1984. *Health Services Administration Education, 1985–87*. Arlington, Va.: Association of University Programs in Health Administration.

Larson, Magali S. 1977. *The Rise of Professionalism: A Sociological Analysis*. Berkeley: University of California Press.

Lawrence, Judith K., and Green, Kenneth C. 1980. *A Question of Quality: The Higher Education Ratings Game*. AAHE-ERIC Higher Education Research Report No. 5. Washington, D.C.: American Association for Higher Education. ED 192 667. 76 pp. MF–$1.00; PC–$9.56.

Leys, Wayne A. R. Summer 1956. "The Terminal Master's Degree." *Harvard Educational Review* 26: 233–40.

McCarty, Donald J. Fall 1979. "Issues in Quality Education and the Evaluation of Nontraditional Graduate Programs." *Alternative Higher Education* 4: 61–69.

Malden, Henry. 1835. *On the Origin of Universities and Academical Degrees*. London: John Taylor.

Malitz, Gerald, ed. 1981. A Classification of Instructional Programs. Washington, D.C.: National Center for Education Statistics.

Marchant, Maurice P., and Wilson, Carolyn F. Summer 1983. "Developing Joint Graduate Programs for Librarians." *Journal of Education for Librarianship* 24: 30–37.

Matchett, W. H. 1980. "Master's Degree Program in Computer Science under Contract to a Large Electronics Firm." *Industry/*

University Cooperative Programs. Proceedings of a workshop. Washington, D.C.: Council of Graduate Schools in the United States. ED 215 612. 127 pp. MF–$1.00; PC–$13.26.

Mayhew, Lewis B. 1970. *Graduate and Professional Education: A Survey of Institutional Plans.* New York: McGraw-Hill.

Mayhew, Lewis B., and Ford, Patrick J. 1974. *Reform in Graduate and Professional Education.* San Francisco: Jossey-Bass.

Midwest College Art Conference. Spring 1965. "Report: The Present Status of the M.F.A. Degree." *Art Journal* 24: 244–49.

Millard, Richard. 1984. "Assessing the Quality of Innovative Graduate Programs." In *Keeping Graduate Programs Responsive to National Needs,* edited by M. Pelczar and L. Solmon. New Directions for Higher Education No. 46. San Francisco: Jossey-Bass.

Miller, John Perry. October 1966. "The Master of Philosophy: A New Degree Is Born." *Journal of Higher Education* 37: 377–81.

Minkel, C. W., and Richards, Mary P. 1986. *Components of Quality in Master's Degree Programs.* Knoxville: Tennessee Conference of Graduate Schools.

Modern Language Association. September 1986a. "Ethnic Studies Programs." *PMLA Directory* 101: 650–51.

———. September 1986b. "Women's Studies Programs." *PMLA Directory* 101: 655–62.

Moyerman, Sue. April 1978. "Relevance of Health Care Administration Curricula." Philadelphia: University of Pennsylvania, Leonard Davis Institute of Health Economics. ED 157 993. 272 pp. MF–$1.00; PC–$23.14.

Murphy, Marion I. 1981. *Master's Programs in Nursing in the Eighties: Trends and Issues.* Washington, D.C.: American Association of Colleges of Nursing.

———. 1985. *Enrollments and Graduation in Baccalaureate and Graduate Programs in Nursing.* Washington, D.C.: American Association of Colleges of Nursing.

Nalbandian, John. 1980. "The Impact of Identity, Competence, and Power Issues in Professional Education Program Design." In *Developing Experiential Learning Programs for Professional Education,* edited by E. T. Byrne and D. E. Wolfe. New Directions for Experiential Learning No. 8. San Francisco: Jossey-Bass.

Nanus, Burt. Spring 1984. "Future Influences on Management Education." *Selections* 1: 15–18.

National Association of Schools of Art and Design. 1985. *Handbook.* Reston, Va.: Author.

National Association of Schools of Dance. 1986. *Handbook 1986–87.* Reston, Va.: Author.

National Association of Schools of Public Affairs and Administration. 1984. *1984 Directory: Programs in Public Affairs and Administration*. Washington, D.C.: Author.

———. 1 September 1986. "Standards for Professional Master's Degree Programs in Public Affairs and Administration." Mimeographed. Washington, D.C.: Author.

National Association of Schools of Theatre. 1983. *Handbook 1984–1985*. Reston, Va.: Author.

National Board of Graduate Education. 1975. *Outlook and Opportunities for Graduate Education: The Final Report with Recommendations*. No. 6. Washington, D.C.: Author. ED 119 568. 84 pp. MF–$1.00; PC–$9.56.

National Center for Education Statistics. 1984. *Trends in Education, 1972–73 to 1992–93*. Washington, D.C.: U.S. Government Printing Office.

———. 1985. "Master's Degrees Conferred by Institutions of Higher Education by Discipline Division, 1970–71 to 1982–83." Washington, D.C.: U.S. Government Printing Office.

National League of Nursing. 1978. *Developing a Master's Program in Nursing*. New York: Author.

———. 1980. *Developing the Functional Role in Master's Education in Nursing*. New York: Author.

———. 1984. *Nursing Student Census with Policy Implications*. New York: Author.

———. 1985. *Master's Education in Nursing: Route to Opportunities in Contemporary Nursing, 1985–86*. New York: NLN, Council of Baccalaureate and Higher Degree Programs.

National Science Foundation. 1982. *Science and Engineering Degrees: 1950–1980*. ED 222 377. 71 pp. MF–$1.00; PC–$7.29.

———. 22 February 1985. "Ph.D. Scientists and Engineers Shift to Industrial Employment and Related Activities." *Science Resource Studies Highlights*. No. 85–301. Washington, D.C.: Author.

Ness, Frederic W., and James, Benjamin D. 1962. *Graduate Study in the Liberal Arts College*. Washington, D.C.: Association of American Colleges.

Nolan, Donald J. 18 August 1986. "Proposed Revisions in the Regulations of the Commissioner of Education Pertaining to Teacher Certification: Announcement of Public Hearing." Unpublished memorandum. Albany, N.Y.: State Education Department.

Nyre, Glenn F., and Reilly, Kathryn C. 1979. *Professional Education in the Eighties: Challenges and Responses*. AAHE-ERIC Higher Education Research Report No. 8. Washington,

D.C.: American Association for Higher Education. ED 179 187.
60 pp. MF–$1.00; PC–$7.29.

Office of Educational Research and Improvement. 1985. "Bachelor's, Master's, and Doctor's Degrees Conferred, by Field, 1982–83." Unpublished data. Washington, D.C.: Author.

Ohio Board of Regents. 1982. *Master Plan for Higher Education: Opportunity in a Time of Change*. Columbus: Author. ED 227 742. 48 pp. MF–$1.00; PC–$5.44.

Oltman, Philip K., and Hartnett, Rodney T. September/October 1985. "The Role of the Graduate Record Examinations in Graduate Admissions." *Journal of Higher Education* 56: 523–37.

Ouchi, William. Autumn 1985. "Reflections on Management Education: Past, Present, and Future." *Selections* 2: 11–18.

Pelczar, Michael, and Frances, Carol. 1984. "Graduate Education: Past Performance and Future Direction." In *Keeping Graduate Programs Responsive to National Needs,* edited by M. Pelczar and L. Solmon. New Directions for Higher Education No. 46. San Francisco: Jossey-Bass.

Pelczar, Michael J., and Solmon, Lewis C., eds. 1984. *Keeping Graduate Programs Responsive to National Needs*. New Directions for Higher Education No. 46. San Francisco: Jossey-Bass.

Pelikan, Jaroslav. 1983. *Scholarship and Its Survival: Questions on the Idea of Graduate Education*. Princeton, N.J.: Princeton University Press.

Peterson, Kent, and Lamont, Valarie C. 1978. "Health Services Research Components of Master's Degree Programs in Health Services Administration." ED 156 004. 75 pp. MF–$1.00; PC–$7.29.

Peterson, Paul V. Winter 1983. "J-School Enrollments Hit Record 91,016." *Journalism Educator* 37: 3–10.
———. Spring 1985. "1984 Survey: No Change in Mass Comm. Enrollments." *Journalism Educator* 40: 3–9.

Pipes, Lana, ed. 1979. *Perspectives on Graduate Programs in Education*. Washington, D.C.: American Association of Colleges for Teacher Education. ED 173 277. 120 pp. MF–$1.00; PC–$11.41.

Plisko, Valena W., and Stern, Joyce D., eds. 1985. *The Condition of Education*. Washington, D.C.: National Center for Education Statistics.

Poppenhagen, Brent W. Fall 1979. "Issues in Alternative Graduate Education." *Alternative Higher Education* 4: 3–11.

Porter, Jack. Spring 1982. "Corporations That Grant Degrees." *Business and Society Review* 41: 41–46.

Rader, Frank J., ed. 1982. *Innovative Graduate Programs Directory*. 4th ed. Saratoga, N.Y.: Empire State College.

Reese, Jack E. May 1967. "New Titles and New Directions in Graduate Education. The Expanded Master's Program at the University of Tennessee." *Journal of Higher Education* 38: 250–56.

Rehder, Robert R. Winter 1982. "SMR Forum—American Business Education: Is It Too Late to Change?" *Sloan Management Review* 21: 63–71.

Ridley, Jack B., and Marchello, Joseph M. April 1985. "Engineering Degrees and Professionalism." *Engineering Education* 75: 650–53.

Roose, M.D., and Anderson, C.J. 1970. *A Rating of Graduate Programs*. Washington, D.C.: American Council on Education.

Roy, Rustum. 1979. "Interdisciplinary Science on Campus: The Elusive Dream." In *Interdisciplinarity and Higher Education*, edited by J. Kockelmans. University Park: Penn State University Press.

Rubin, Allen. 1985. "Statistics on Social Work Education in the United States: 1984." Washington, D.C.: CSWE.

Ruud, Millard H. 1985. "Graduate Study in an Area of Concentration." Mimeographed. Washington, D.C.: Association of American Law Schools.

Ryan, Michael. 1980. *Journalism Education at the Master's Level*. Journalism Monographs No. 66. Association for Education in Journalism. ED 186 903. 48 pp. MF–$1.00; PC–$5.44.

Sandler, Irving. Spring 1982. "The School of Art at Yale, 1950–1970: The Collective Reminiscences of Twenty Distinguished Alumni." *Art Journal* 42: 14–21.

Santora, Dolores. 1980. *Conceptual Frameworks Used in Baccalaureate and Master's Degree Curricula*. New York: National League of Nursing.

Schein, Edgar H. 1972. *Professional Education: Some New Directions*. New York: McGraw-Hill.

Schmotter, James W. Spring 1984. "Interview with Professor James E. Howell." *Selections* 1: 9–14.

Schneider, Ann. 1985. "Center Graduates: Their Disciplines and Career Choices." Mimeographed. Washington, D.C.: United States Department of Education.

Schuster, Marilyn R., and Van Dyne, Susan R. 1984. "Project on Women and Social Change: Smith College." In *Toward a Balanced Curriculum*, edited by B. Spanier, A. Bloom, and D. Boroviak. Cambridge, Mass.: Schenkman Publishing Co.

Smartt, Steven. 1984. "Linking Program Reviews to the Budget." In *Financial Incentives for Academic Quality*, edited by

J. Folger. New Directions for Higher Education No. 48. San Francisco: Jossey-Bass.

Smith, Mary Howard, ed. 1981. *Graduate Education in Nursing: Issues and Future Directions*. Atlanta: Southern Regional Education Board. ED 210 972. 59 pp. MF–$1.00; PC–$7.29.

Snell, John L. 1965. "The Master's Degree." In *Graduate Education Today,* edited by E. Walters. Washington, D.C.: American Council on Education.

Solmon, Lewis C. 1984. "A Theory of Innovation in Graduate Education." In *Keeping Graduate Programs Responsive to National Needs,* edited by M. J. Pelczar and L. C. Solmon. New Directions for Higher Education No. 46. San Francisco: Jossey-Bass.

Spruell, Geraldine. October 1985. "Two Degrees of Distinction." *Training and Development Journal* 39: 59–65.

Spurr, Stephen H. 1970. *Academic Degree Structures: Innovative Approaches. Principles of Reform in Degree Structures in the United States*. Berkeley, Cal.: Carnegie Foundation for the Advancement of Teaching.

Stark, Joan S., and Austin, Ann E. 1982. "Recipients of Master's Degrees in Education at the University of Michigan. A Career Follow-Up Study." ED 253 500. 87 pp. MF–$1.00; PC–$9.56.

Steele, John E., and Ward, Lewis B. January/February 1974. "M.B.A.s: Mobile, Well-Situated, Well-Paid." *Harvard Business Review* 52: 99–110.

Stolzenberg, Ross M. Spring 1985. "The Changing Demand for Graduate Management Education." *Selections* 2: 10–24.

Storr, Richard J. 1953. *The Beginning of Graduate Education in America*. Chicago: University of Chicago Press.

———. 1973. *The Beginning of the Future: A Historical Approach to Graduate Education in Arts and Science*. New York: McGraw-Hill.

Thomas, Flavel S. 1898. *A Dictionary of University Degrees*. New York: C. W. Bardeen.

Tucker, Allan, and Mautz, Robert B. Summer 1985. "Queuing up for Quality: The Politics of Graduate Programming." *Educational Record* 66: 11–14.

Turmeau, W. A. July 1982. "Engineering Degree Curricula for the Future." *Higher Education* 11: 397–403.

Veysey, Laurence R. 1965. *The Emergence of the American University*. Chicago: University of Chicago Press.

Webster, David S. 1979. "How to Assess Quality in Master's Degree Programs: A New and Better Way." College Park, Md.: University of Maryland. ED 185 916. 12 pp. MF–$1.00; PC not available EDRS.

————. 1985. "Institutional Effectiveness Using Scholarly Peer Assessments as Major Criteria." *Review of Higher Education* 9: 67–82.

Western Interstate Commission for Higher Education. 1985. *Inventory of Graduate Programs in the Northwest*. Boulder, Colo.: Author.

Whaley, W. G. Winter 1966. "American Academic Degrees." *Educational Record* 47: 525–37.

Wild, Cheryl L.; Fortna, Richard; and Knapp, Jean. 1978. *Development of a System for the Empirical Determination of Issues in Postsecondary Education*. Vol. 1 and 2. Princeton, N.J.: Educational Testing Service. ED 162 557. 650 pp. MF–$1.32; PC–$48.10.

Willenbrock, F. Karl. 1985. "The Status of Engineering Education in the United States." In *The State of Graduate Education,* edited by B. L. R. Smith. Washington, D.C.: The Brookings Institution.

Wilson, Louis R. 1970. "Historical Development of Education for Librarianship in the United States." In *Education for Librarianship,* edited by B. Berelson. Reprint. Freeport, N.Y.: Books for Libraries Press.

Wolfe, Douglas E., and Byrne, Eugene T. 1980. "An Experiential M.B.A. Program: Results of an Experiment." In *Developing Experiential Learning Programs for Professional Education,* edited by E. T. Byrne and D. E. Wolfe. New Directions for Experiential Learning No. 8. San Francisco: Jossey-Bass.

Yager, Robert. October 1982. "The Status of Science Education Programs at Graduate Institutions Offering Only the Master's Degree." *Science Education* 66: 693–97.

Young, Kenneth E.; Chambers, Charles M.; Kells, H. R.; and associates. 1983. *Understanding Accreditation*. San Francisco: Jossey-Bass.

Yungmyer, Elinor. Fall 1984. "Accreditation in the Field of Library and Information Science." *Journal of Education for Library and Information Science* 25: 109–17.

Zottoli, John V. 1984. "Self-Directed Learning in Public Management Master's Programs." D.P.A. dissertation, University of Southern California.

INDEX

American Association of Colleges of Teacher Education
  (AACTE), 50
American Association of Library Schools (AALS), 66
American Association of Schools of Social Work (AASSW), 72
American Bar Association (ABA), 66
American Council on Education (ACE), 16, 30
American Institute of Certified Public Accountants, 43
American Library Association (ALA), 67, 68
American Nursing Association (ANA), 58
American Physical Therapy Association, 62
American Public Works Association (APWA), 71
American Society for Engineering Education (ASEE), 53, 54
American Society of Newspaper Editors, 64
ANA (see American Nursing Association)
Antioch College: cooperative education, 81
APWA (see American Public Works Association)
Architecture as a field of study, 56
Art/design as a field of study, 56
Arthur D. Little Management Education Institute, 40
Articulation: undergraduate/graduate, 9, 73
ASEE (see American Society for Engineering Education)
Assistantships, 14
Associate of Arts (A.A.), 72
Association for Media-based Continuing Research for
  Engineers, 39
Association of American Universities (AAU), 8, 9, 10, 67
Association of Graduate Schools (AGS), 10, 31
Association of University Programs in Health Administration, 61

B
B.A. (see Bachelor of Arts)
B.L.S. (see Bachelor of Library Science)
B.S.N. (see Bachelor of Science in Nursing)
B.S.W. (see Bachelor of Social Work)
Bachelor of Arts (B.A.)
        combined degree, 18
        degrees conferred, 50
        financial status, 48
        first, 16
Bachelor of Laws (LL.B.), 65, 66
Bachelor of Library Science (B.L.S.), 67
Bachelor of Science in Nursing (B.S.N.), 60
Bachelor of Social Work (B.S.W.), 72, 73, 74
Bachelor's degree
        decline in awards, 51
        devaluation, 25
        entry-level credential, 31

Fortune 500 executives, 42
Fund for the Advancement of Education, 10

G
General education, 8
General Motors Institute of Engineering and Management, 39
Georgia: program discontinuance, 49
GMAT scores, 42
Government regulation/policy, 33
GPSA (see Graduate Program Self-Assessment Service)
Graduate Program Self-Assessment Service (GPSA), 31, 85
Graduate Record Exam (GRE), 65
Graduate Record Examination Board (GREB), 27, 30, 31
Graduate schools (see also Professional programs)
  accreditation standards, 37
  expansion, 37–38
Graduate schools of education (GSE), 45, 46, 47
Graduate studies program, 80
Graduation requirements, 39
Grants, 14
GRE (see Graduate Record Exam)
GREB (see Graduate Record Examination Board)
GSE (see Graduate schools of education)

H
Harvard University
  first degrees, 7, 16, 37
  law degrees, 65
  M.A.T., 47
  new master's, 63
  teachers' seminary, 45
Hawaii: mandated fifth-year master's, 43
Health professions, 36, 41, 58–63
Health services administration as a field of study, 61–63
History as a field of study, 30
Holmes Group, 47, 48, 52
Home economics as a field of study, 36
Hotel/motel management as a field of study, 38
Human services as a field of study, 51
Humanities, 31

I
Indiana University: library science, 68
Indices of quality, 27
Industry–university cooperation, 44
Inservice teacher training, 52

Insurance as a field of study, 38
Interdisciplinary degree, 62, 78
International education as a field of study, 63–64
International management as a field of study, 40
Internships
    fine arts, 57
    interdisciplinary programs, 80
    part of two-year programs, 69
    rehabilitation counseling, 62
    teaching, 47, 49
Introductory courses, 17
Inventories of master's degrees, 81
Investment as a field of study, 38
Iowa State University
    graduate studies program, 80
    writing programs, 57
Iowa Writers Workshop, 57

J
J.D. (see Juris Doctor)
Job market (see Labor market)
Joint degrees, 18, 32, 33, 41, 67–68, 71, 75
Journalism as a field of study, 21, 64–65
Juris Doctor (J.D.)
    as joint degree, 18, 41, 64, 75
    first-professional degree, 65
    nomenclature, 86
    prestige, 25

K
Kennedy School of Government, 63

L
Labor market, 14, 55, 60, 67
Land grant universities, 47
Language fluency
    Latin/Greek, 7
    master's requirement, 11
Lanier, Judith, 47
Latin American studies, 64
Law as a field of study, 18, 23, 24, 65–66
Legislative proposal, 43
Liberal arts
    graduates enrolling in professional programs, 32
    master's degrees, 11, 12
Library science as a field of study, 21, 66–69

Licensing, 7, 21, 45
LL.B. (see Bachelor of Laws)
LL.M. (see Master of Laws)
Loans, 14

M
M.A. (see Master of Arts)
M.A.L.D. (see Master of Arts in Law and Diplomacy)
M.A.L.I.R. (see Master of Law in Labor and Industrial
  Relations)
M.A.L.S. (see Master of Arts in Liberal Studies; Master of
  Asian Law)
M.A.T. (see Master of Arts in Teaching)
M.B.A. (see Master of Business Administration)
M.C.J. (see Master of Comparative Jurisprudence)
M.C.L. (see Master of Comparative Law)
M.D. (see Doctor of Medicine)
M.E. (see Master of Engineering)
M.Ed. (see Master of Education)
M.F.A. (see Master of Fine Arts)
M.L.I. (see Master of Arts or Science in Legal Institutions)
M.L.S. (see Master of Library Science)
M.M. (see Master of Management; Master of Music)
M.M.E. (see Master of Mechanical Engineering)
M.M.P.A. (see Master of Municipal Public Administration)
M.N. (see Master of Nursing)
M.P.A. (see Master of Public Administration)
M.P.H. (see Master of Public Health)
M.P.L. (see Master of Urban Planning)
M.P.P. (see Master of Public Policy)
M.Phil. (see Master of Philosophy)
M.S. (see Master of Science)
M.S.G. (see Master of Science in Gerontology)
M.S.I.M. (see Master of Science in Industrial Management)
M.S.I.S. (see Master of Science in Information Science)
M.S.M. (see Master of Science in Management)
M.S.N. (see Master of Science in Nursing)
M.S.W. (see Master of Social Work)
M.U.A. (see Master of Urban Affairs)
Management as a field of study, 37
Management training, 40
Marketing as a field of study, 37, 38
Mass communications as a field of study, 64–65
Massachusetts: first-year teacher licensing, 48
Massachusetts General Hospital, 60
Massachusetts Institute of Technology (MIT): M.S.M., 40
Master of Arts (M.A.)

Master of Social Work (M.S.W.), 48, 72, 73, 74, 75
Master of Software Engineering, 39
Master of Urban Affairs (M.U.A.), 70
Master of Urban Planning (M.P.L.), 75
Master of Urban Systems Engineering, 54
Master teacher, 7, 48
Master's degrees
     ambiguity in meaning, 85
     enrollment trends, 50–52
     inventories of, 81
     number of people holding, 25
     signify professionalism, 83
Mathematics as a field of study, 37
Medical school curricular model, 20
Medicine as a field of study, 18, 23, 24
Medieval university, 7
Mentor relationship, 56
Merit pay, 49
MGH Institute of Health Professions, 60
Minority groups, 46
MIT (see Massachusetts Institute of Technology)
Music as a field of study, 56, 57
Morrill Act of 1862, 7, 53

N
NASAD (see National Association of Schools of Art and Design)
NASPAA (see National Association of Schools of Public Affairs
   and Administration)
National Association of Schools of Theatre, 57
National Association of Schools of Art and Design (NASAD), 56
National Association of Schools of Public Affairs and Administra-
   tion (NASPAA), 69, 70, 71
National Association of Social Work, 72
National Association of State Directors of Teacher Education and
   Certification, 23
National Board of Graduate Education, 84
National Council for Accreditation of Teacher Education
   (NCATE), 23, 50
National Institutes of Health (NIH), 63
National League of Nursing (NLN), 58, 59, 61
National Teachers' Examination Core Battery, 49
National Technological University, 39, 55
NCATE (see National Council for Accreditation of Teacher
   Education)
New England Association of Schools and Colleges, 40
New Jersey: first-year teacher licensing, 48

University of Illinois: student objectives, 43
University of Maryland: program review, 31
University of Michigan
 graduate surveys, 52
 two-year M.S., 40
University of Minnesota: first school of nursing, 58
University of South Carolina: delivery systems, 81
University of Tennessee: nursing program, 60

V
Vanderbilt University: library science, 67
Visual arts as a field of study, 56
Vocationalism, 38

W
Wang Institute of Graduate Studies, 39, 40, 55
Washington: teacher certification, 49
Weekend program, 71
Wesleyan University: M.A.L.S., 79
Western Interstate Commission for Higher Education
 (WICHE), 81
WICHE (see Western Interstate Commission for Higher
 Education)
Wilson Foundation, 68
Women
 M.B.A. programs, 38
 M.S.W. programs, 73
 professional degree programs, 3, 14, 22, 46, 51, 55
Women's studies, 78–79
Woodrow Wilson School of Public and International Affairs, 63
World War II, 10
Writing programs, 57

Y
Yale School of Art, 58
Yale University, 11, 44

3–2 model program, 64
4–1 model program, 47, 72
4–2 model program, 47

ASHE-ERIC HIGHER EDUCATION REPORTS

Starting in 1983, the Association for the Study of Higher Education assumed cosponsorship of the Higher Education Reports with the ERIC Clearinghouse on Higher Education. For the previous 11 years, ERIC and the American Association for Higher Education prepared and published the reports.

Each report is the definitive analysis of a tough higher education problem, based on a thorough research of pertinent literature and institutional experiences. Report topics, identified by a national survey, are written by noted practitioners and scholars with prepublication manuscript reviews by experts.

Eight monographs (10 monographs before 1985) in the ASHE-ERIC Higher Education Report series are published each year, available individually or by subscription. Subscription to eight issues is $60 regular; $50 for members of AERA, AAHE, and AIR; $40 for members of ASHE. (Add $7.50 outside the United States.)

Prices for single copies, including 4th class postage and handling, are $10.00 regular and $7.50 for members of AERA, AAHE, AIR, and ASHE ($7.50 regular and $6.00 for members for 1983 and 1984 reports, $6.50 regular and $5.00 for members for reports published before 1983). If faster 1st class postage is desired for U.S. and Canadian orders, add $.75 for each publication ordered; overseas, add $4.50. For VISA and MasterCard payments, include card number, expiration date, and signature. Orders under $25 must be prepaid. Bulk discounts are available on orders of 15 or more reports (not applicable to subscriptions). Order from the Publications Department, Association for the Study of Higher Education, One Dupont Circle, Suite 630, Washington, D.C. 20036, 202/296-2597. Write for a publication list of all the Higher Education Reports available.

1986 Higher Education Reports

1. Post-tenure Faculty Evaluation: Threat or Opportunity?
   Christine M. Licata

2. Blue Ribbon Commissions and Higher Education: Changing Academe from the Outside
   Janet R. Johnson and Laurence R. Marcus

3. Responsive Professional Education: Balancing Outcomes and Opportunities
   Joan S. Stark, Malcolm A. Lowther, and Bonnie M.K. Hagerty

4. Increasing Students' Learning: A Faculty Guide to Reducing Stress among Students
   Neal A. Whitman, David C. Spendlove, and Claire H. Clark

5. Student Financial Aid and Women: Equity Dilemma?
   Mary Moran

6. The Master's Degree: Tradition, Diversity, Innovation
   Judith S. Glazer

1985 Higher Education Reports

1. Flexibility in Academic Staffing: Effective Policies and Practices
   Kenneth P. Mortimer, Marque Bagshaw, and Andrew T. Masland

---

The Master's Degree

2. Associations in Action: The Washington, D.C., Higher
   Education Community
   Harland G. Bloland

3. And on the Seventh Day: Faculty Consulting and Supplemental
   Income
   Carol M. Boyer and Darrell R. Lewis

4. Faculty Research Performance: Lessons from the Sciences and
   Social Sciences
   John W. Creswell

5. Academic Program Reviews: Institutional Approaches, Expectations,
   and Controversies
   Clifton F. Conrad and Richard F. Wilson

6. Students in Urban Settings: Achieving the Baccalaureate Degree
   Richard C. Richardson, Jr., and Louis W. Bender

7. Serving More Than Students: A Critical Need for College Student
   Personnel Services
   Peter H. Garland

8. Faculty Participation in Decision Making: Necessity or Luxury?
   Carol E. Floyd

1984 Higher Education Reports

1. Adult Learning: State Policies and Institutional Practices
   K. Patricia Cross and Anne-Marie McCartan

2. Student Stress: Effects and Solutions
   Neal A. Whitman, David C. Spendlove, and Claire H. Clark

3. Part-time Faculty: Higher Education at a Crossroads
   Judith M. Gappa

4. Sex Discrimination Law in Higher Education: The Lessons of the
   Past Decade
   *J. Ralph Lindgren, Patti T. Ota, Perry A. Zirkel, and
   Nan Van Gieson*

5. Faculty Freedoms and Institutional Accountability: Interactions and
   Conflicts
   Steven G. Olswang and Barbara A. Lee

6. The High-Technology Connection: Academic/Industrial Cooperation
   for Economic Growth
   Lynn G. Johnson

7. Employee Educational Programs: Implications for Industry and
   Higher Education
   Suzanne·W. Morse

8. Academic Libraries: The Changing Knowledge Centers of Colleges
   and Universities
   Barbara B. Moran

9. Futures Research and the Strategic Planning Process: Implications for
   Higher Education
   James L. Morrison, William L. Renfro, and Wayne I. Boucher

10. Faculty Workload: Research, Theory, and Interpretation
    Harold E. Yuker

1983 Higher Education Reports

1. The Path to Excellence: Quality Assurance in Higher Education
   Laurence R. Marcus, Anita O. Leone, and Edward D. Goldberg

2. Faculty Recruitment, Retention, and Fair Employment: Obligations and Opportunities
   John S. Waggaman

3. Meeting the Challenges: Developing Faculty Careers
   Michael C. T. Brookes and Katherine L. German

4. Raising Academic Standards: A Guide to Learning Improvement
   Ruth Talbott Keimig

5. Serving Learners at a Distance: A Guide to Program Practices
   Charles E. Feasley

6. Competence, Admissions, and Articulation: Returning to the Basics in Higher Education
   Jean L. Preer

7. Public Service in Higher Education: Practices and Priorities
   Patricia H. Crosson

8. Academic Employment and Retrenchment: Judicial Review and Administrative Action
   Robert M. Hendrickson and Barbara A. Lee

9. Burnout: The New Academic Disease
   Winifred Albizu Meléndez and Rafael M. de Guzmán

10. Academic Workplace: New Demands, Heightened Tensions
    Ann E. Austin and Zelda F. Gamson

NOTES